THE ELEGANT LIFE OF THE CHINESE LITERATI

長物志

From the Chinese Classic,
Treatise on Superfluous Things

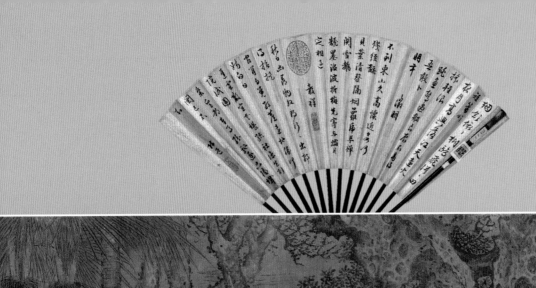

THE ELEGANT LIFE OF THE CHINESE LITERATI 長物志

From the Chinese Classic, *Treatise on Superfluous Things*

Finding Harmony and Joy in Everyday Objects

By Wen Zhenheng
Translated by Tony Blishen
With a Foreword by Craig Clunas

Better Link Press

Fig. 1 *The Cassia Grove Studio* (detail)
Wen Zhengming (1470–1559)
Color on paper
Height 31.6 cm × Width 56.2 cm
Metropolitan Museum of Art
New York

Wen Zhengming was one of the Ming dynasty's great masters of painting and calligraphy. He was also the great-grandfather of Wen Zhenheng. In this picture, executed following his resignation from office and return to Suzhou, a mountain retreat nestles in the tree shade, its back to the mountain and facing water, the railed enclosure indicating the presence of water to one side of the retreat. The sight of the master of the retreat standing gazing at the landscape of lakes and mountains while a boy attendant awaits instructions creates a sense of the refined elegance that belonged to the class of gentleman scholar.

On page 1
Fig. 2 *The Garden of the Humble Administrator,* Album Leaf
Wen Zhengming
Ink on paper
Height 26.4 cm × Width 27.3 cm
Metropolitan Museum of Art
New York

A scholar sits on a bank overlooking the water beside an ancient tree with a thatched hut behind him, there is no ornamentation and the atmosphere is one of tranquil detachment. Further information on this album may be found on pages 58 and 150.

This book is edited and designed by the Editorial Committee of *Cultural China* series.

Text by Wen Zhenheng
Translation by Tony Blishen
Cover Design by Wang Wei
Interior Design by Li Jing and Hu Bin (Yuan Yinchang Design Studio)

Copy Editor: Diane Davies
Editorial Assistant: Pei Zhuomin
Editor: Wu Yuezhou
Editorial Director: Zhang Yicong

Senior Consultants: Sun Yong, Wu Ying, Yang Xinci
Managing Director and Publisher: Wang Youbu

ISBN: 978-1-60220-039-5

Address any comments about *The Elegant Life of the Chinese Literati* to:

Better Link Press
99 Park Ave
New York, NY 10016
USA

or

Shanghai Press and Publishing Development Co., Ltd.
F 7 Donghu Road, Shanghai, China (200031)
Email: comments_betterlinkpress@hotmail.com

Printed in China by Shenzhen Donnelley Printing Co., Ltd.

1 3 5 7 9 10 8 6 4 2

Part of the author's fee for this book has been assigned to the China Written Works Copyright Society for payment, with whom the relevant copyright holders are requested to make contact.

Quanjing provides the images on pages 21, 24, 27–28, 33, 46, 50, 74, 103, 105, 138–141 and 148–149.
Plant Photo Bank of China (PPBC) provides the images on pages 32, 34–37, 39–40, 136–137 and 139–140.

CONTENTS

Fig. 11 *A Complete View of the Scenery of Suzhou* (detail)

Shen Zhou (1427–1509)
Height 41.9 cm × Length 1749.3 cm
Palace Museum, Taibei

In this long hand scroll, Shen Zhou has drawn upon the experience of his own travels to present a skilful portrayal of the scenic spots and historical sites that lie scattered between the town of Suzhou and Lake Taihu, indicating the general topography of the area. The detail here is of the portion of the scroll that covers a view of Tiger Hill. Wen Zhenheng, the author of the *Treatise on Superfluous Things*, was a native of Suzhou.

FOREWORD

For the imperial librarians of the Qing dynasty (1644–1911) in the eighteenth century, it was the edifying end made by Wen Zhenheng (1585–1645) which was the saving grace of a life otherwise rather over-devoted to the trivial. They were less impressed by his minute attention to the details of tables and chairs and water pots and flowers and hats than they were by the heroism which led him to starve to death rather than live under the Manchu emperors who they themselves served. His heroic martyrdom was set alongside his descent from one of the most elevated and successful families of Ming dynasty (1368–1644) China; he was the great-grandson of the famous calligrapher, painter, and all-round paragon of literati accomplishments Wen Zhengming (1470–1559), while his elder brother Wen Zhenmeng (1574–1636) rose to the very highest ranks of the imperial bureaucracy, as a Grand Secretary and the man whose job it was to personally lecture a youthful emperor on the meaning of the Confucian Classics. Wen Zhenheng himself achieved no such public renown in his lifetime, but at the same time he was a prominent member of a wealthy and well-connected family, who spent time in a series of ill-defined government posts, some with cultural connotations as editor or calligrapher. In his *Treatise on Superfluous Things*, here presented for the first time in a complete English translation, he is happy to let drop occasional statements which reveal his proximity to imperial power and grandeur, as for example when he mentions that "I once saw a piece of water-worn agarwood incense … carved with a pattern of dragons and phoenix in the ancestral temple dedicated by the Ming Emperor Shizong (1507–1567) to his father,"

This painting portrays an elegant assembly of the eighteen scholars. The liveliness of facial expression and the vigor of the fine linear patterning of their costumes fully expresses the elegance of spirit and posture associated with the gentleman scholar class. The painting also illustrates the furniture, literary impedimenta, arrangement and ornamentation and costumes favored by the literati.

or when he provides the delicious sense of access to insider information with, "The Palace Manufactory produces an incense coil called 'hanging dragon' which burns suspended, the frame from which it hangs is very unusual." Here, we are told quite firmly, is someone who *knows*. He portrays his knowledge as both deep and extensive, whether in the lengthy lists of artists' names, or the precise contexts in which the lacquered wares of Japan (mentioned with surprising frequency) are acceptable for storing their works. But be warned; blame is dished out as often as praise, and "Lacquered desks are vulgar in the extreme." You have been warned.

The *Zhang Wu Zhi*, which can probably be dated to a period when its author was still in his early thirties i.e. about 1615–1620, was first given its English title as *Treatise on Superfluous Things* by the great Dutch sinologist Robert van Gulik (1910–1967), who translated the "Hanging Paintings According to the Season" section of the "Calligraphy and Painting" Chapter in his 1958 work, *Chinese Pictorial Art as Viewed by the Connoisseur*. Van Gulik identifies Wen Zhenheng's *Treatise* as one of a number of books written in China in the commercially vibrant, culturally febrile late Ming which aim to lay down the law as to the life the gentleman should live, and what aspects of the rich material culture of the age he should surround himself with, and which shun. So the *Treatise* is not exactly unique, it sits alongside books like *Eight Discourses on the Art of Living*, by the wealthy merchant and playwright Gao Lian (Ming dynasty), published in Wen's childhood, in 1591. However the *Treatise* is singular, in that concentrates entirely on the material world of things which the man of taste is to have around him. It excludes the kinds of materials on the care of the self and the prolongation of life through exercise which are of such concern to Gao Lian, although its attention to fruits

and vegetables as the only kinds of foodstuffs it discusses (alongside tea) suggests that the fastidious Wen Zhenheng *was* interested in how to look after yourself in terms of diet. While it does deal with antiques of various kinds, from painting and calligraphy to bronzes, ceramics and jades, the majority of its entries deal with contemporary objects, a fact which distinguishes the *Treatise* from a work like the early Ming *Essential Criteria of Antiquities* by Cao Zhao (1388), which seems to aim more at the collector. It is rather the sense of access to life as it was lived (admittedly a very male life and one restricted to a few rich men at that) which gives the book you hold much of its charm today, as in the entry on how to get your servants to teach the tame cranes in your garden to dance. There are wealthy collectors today who have taken the *Treatise* almost as a shopping list of desirable objects; I'm not sure if any of them have actually tried the crane-training techniques laid out here.

One of the things I have often been asked by students, in introducing them to the world of Wen Zhenheng, is whether his *Treatise* exists to bring new sorts of consumers into the fold of elegance, by explaining what to have and what not to have, or whether on the contrary it exists to *exclude*, by creating a set of rules so complex, so inflected by time and place and circumstance that the players can never get it right. As he says himself at one point, "sticking rigidly to the rules results in vulgarity." Only anxiety is generated by the fact that the player of the game can never win. Now thanks to Tony Blishen's care and energy as a translator, readers of English can, if only in the imagination, play the game for themselves.

Craig Clunas
Oxford
May 4th 2019

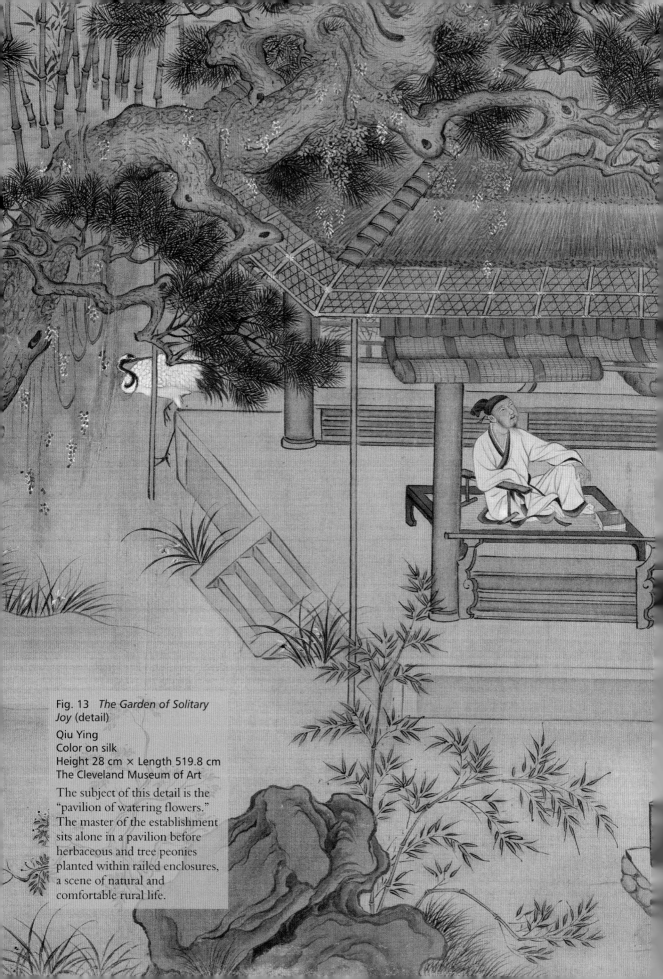

Fig. 13 *The Garden of Solitary
Joy* (detail)

Qiu Ying
Color on silk
Height 28 cm × Length 519.8 cm
The Cleveland Museum of Art

The subject of this detail is the
"pavilion of watering flowers."
The master of the establishment
sits alone in a pavilion before
herbaceous and tree peonies
planted within railed enclosures,
a scene of natural and
comfortable rural life.

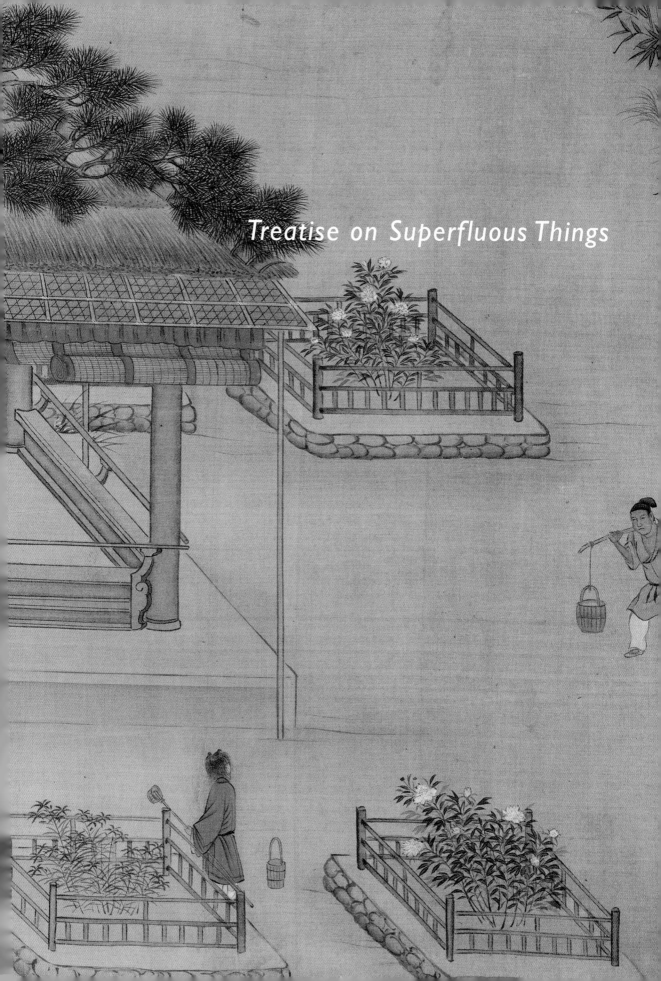

Treatise on Superfluous Things

FOREWORD

Fig. 15 *Spirit of the Poetry of Tao Yuanming* (detail)
Shi Tao (1641–c. 1718)
Ink and color on paper
Height 27 cm × Width 21.3 cm
Palace Museum, Beijing

This 12-leaf album is based upon the poetry of Tao Yuanming in its reflection of the beauty and natural quality of rural life. This is the sixth leaf in the album and depicts an old man clad in a plain wide cloth gown standing at the edge of a stream and gazing at the unpeopled scenery as if deep in thoughts of remote antiquity. The artist also employs this tableau to express approval of a philosophy of life that values detachment from the world, indifference to wealth and glory and contentment with one's lot and the dispositions of fate.

An appreciation of the tranquility of woods and valleys, the tasting of wine and tea, the collection and arrangement of pictures and books and of vessels may, in life in general, be regarded as a matter of leisurely elegance but in ordinary matters it may be superfluous. How is it that knowledgeable people can, on this basis, form an estimate of a person's character, and reach a judgment of their taste, talent and sensibility? It is as if there are people who absorb all the spirit of beauty past and present available to the senses, who assemble all the curios in the world for their own delectation, and clasping this apparel that cannot keep out the cold, those food vessels that cannot assuage hunger and, valuing them more highly than a two-handed jade disc or gold and riches, recklessly take them as an expression of their own extraordinary generosity and loftiness of spirit; yet without the true taste, true talent and true sensibility to master it all, their style and taste cannot be the same.

Of late, there have been some sons of the rich and a handful of the ignorant, uncouth

and stupid, who, regarding themselves as fine fellows, no sooner open their mouths at a meeting of connoisseurs than they spew forth vulgarity, their handling of objects is clumsy, they indulge in exaggerated gestures of appreciation, they are full of insult for the refined, so much so that gentlemen of true taste, talent and sensibility avoid discussion of matters of style and elegance. Oh, that there should be such excess! Consider the Western Han dynasty (206 BC–AD 25) essayist and poet Sima Xiangru (179–118 BC) who sold his carriages and horses and bought a tavern with Zhuo Wenjun (175–121 BC) who, clad in an apron, worked rinsing wine vessels; or the Eastern Jin dynasty (317–420) poet Tao Yuanming (365 or 372 or 376–427) with more than ten *mu* (roughly 6,000 m^2) of land and property and eight or nine thatched huts set amidst chrysanthemums and pines, who took wine when he could; their situations were far

Fig. 14 *Eighteen Scholars Screen*
Du Jin (1456–after 1528)
Ink and color on silk
Height 134.2 cm × Width 78.6 cm
Shanghai Museum

Mastery of the four arts of "playing the *qin* (zither, see note on page 108), chess, calligraphy and painting" was, from ancient times, a necessary achievement for a scholar. During the Zhenguan era (627–649) of the Tang dynasty (618–907) there was the tale of the eighteen scholars, well versed in history ancient and modern and of sound political judgment, who assisted Li Shimin, the Tang Emperor Taizong (598–649) and made an outstanding contribution to the glory of the era. Historically, this has provided subject matter for paintings. This is the panel from the screen representing calligraphy.

Fig. 16   Copy of Wang Wei's *The Wang River Estate* (detail)

Anon. (Ming dynasty), attributed to Song Xu (1525–c. 1606), formerly attributed to Wang Meng (1301 or 1308–1385)
Ink and color on silk
Height 30 cm × Length 1075.6 cm
The Freer and Sackler Galleries, Washington D.C.

In his later years the poet Wang Wei lived in seclusion at his Wang River estate in the foothills south of Xi'an where he created a series of paintings known as *The Wang River Estate* and became the first to advocate the principle of poetry and painting taking equal place in a work of art. The original is no longer extant. In a development that became a tradition in the art of Chinese gardens, he integrated the conceptual ideas of painting with garden layout and creative landscaping to "take the painting to the garden so that the painting turns to scenery." This picture is one of a number of copies that are still extant. In it, gazebos, terraces, multistoried and waterside pavilions appear here and there amongst the hills and streams and people are seen playing chess, taking wine and participating in drinking games. It is Wang Wei's ideal of rural life.

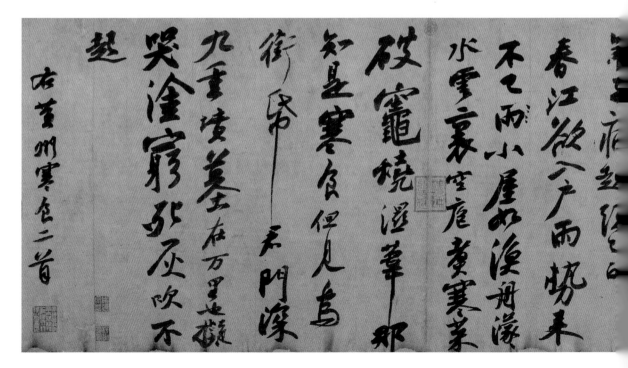

apart but they were as one in spirit (fig. 15). The Tang dynasty artist and poet Wang Wei (?701–761) lived simply with only a camp bed and books, brewed tea and pounded herbs in a mortar (fig. 16); the Tang dynasty poet Bai Juyi (772–846), possessor of singing girls and fine horses and strange stones from Xishan Mountain (in present Suzhou), who built a hermit cell in Lushan; the Northern Song dynasty (960–1127) poet Su Shi (1037–1101) who took singing girls on drunken trips on the West Lake and visited the Red Cliffs (in present Hubei Province) by boat and who caroused with his drinking companion Abbot Foyin at Snow Lodge (fig. 17); all of them differed as between extravagance and frugality but without damaging their cultivation of self and without obliterating their taste and talents or concealing their true self and style.

I have always held this view and told others of it, but only my friend Wen Zhenheng entirely agrees with me. In the coming spring his compilation, *Treatise on Superfluous Things* (*Zhang Wu Zhi*) in twelve parts will appear before the literary and artistic public and he has entrusted me with the writing of a foreword. The studios and retreats I see in this book of Mr. Wen's are ordered, precious in their superiority and beauty, their simplicity and

Fig. 17 *Three Years of Fasting on Cold Food* (detail)
Su Shi
Ink on plain paper (seventeen lines of semi-cursive script, 129 characters in all)
Height 18.9 cm × Width 34.2 cm
Palace Museum, Taibei

Su Shi was a Song dynasty literary figure, a calligrapher and artist and poet of brilliant achievements. This inscription was written when he was in exile from the court and is filled with a feeling of the passing of seasons, the difficulties of life, and the setbacks of an official career. The calligraphy is unrestrained in spirit and is considered the finest extant example of Su Shi's work.

Fig. 18 *The Peach Blossom Spring* (detail)
Anon. (Ming dynasty), attributed to Qiu Ying
(c. 1501–c. 1551)
Ink and color on paper
Height 33 cm × Length 472 cm
Museum of Fine Arts, Boston

The subject matter of this painting is drawn from
the Eastern Jin dynasty poet Tao Yuanming's poem
Record of the Peach Blossom Spring (*Tao Hua Yuan Ji*)
and depicts the joy of living in seclusion, a part of
the ideal life of a scholar. The painting perfectly
combines people with place to create an earthly
fairyland of elegant scenery and relaxed leisure.

purity; flowers and trees, water and rocks,
birds and fish, are lifelike and precious in their
grace and remoteness and all attractively in
harmony; calligraphy and paintings are well
set out, precious in their wonder and rarity
and perpetuity; tables and couches accord
with the rules, vessels and utensils have form,
placing and arrangement are appropriately
determined, all precious in essence, suitability
and selection, both simple and natural; clothing
and adornment have the fashionable look of
the Jin dynasty (265–420) (whose worthies
affected a conscious elegance and wore
capacious outer garments), boats and carriages
seem appropriate to the fairy garden of Wuling
(fig. 18) and take account of the difficulties of
the road to Shu, vegetables and fruit have the
scent of melons and dates in a fairy garden.
Incense and tea encompass the addictive habits
of the Three Kingdoms (220–280) strategist
Xun Yu (163–212) and the Tang dynasty poet
Lu Tong (c. 775–835). Incense and tea are

precious in their remoteness and lightness of
taste, they hold an aftertaste in perpetuity (Xun
Yu was addicted to incense and it is said that
the fragrance of incense did not disperse from
the places where he sat for three days; Lu Tong
was expert in the tasting of tea and was called
the Immortal of Tea) (fig. 19). Convention
decrees that as a whole our decorative leisure
activities should convey a sense of frugality
and simplicity throughout and encourage the
abandonment of extravagance. It is not only the
ignorant and stupid that cannot comprehend
this truth; even those gentlemen of true taste,
talent and sensibility, who seek the strange and
novel should bow in respect to Wen Zhenheng
as the fortress that protects them. Not only
has the world a new book, but for our band of
literary gentlemen it is an event as well!

Consequently, I said to Wen Zhenheng,
"Your august forbear, the Grand Scribe
Wen Zhengming's reverence for antiquity
was preeminent throughout the land of Wu
(the delta of the Yangtze River) for nigh on
a century and the family reputation spread
far and wide. The saying 'There is painting
in poetry and poetry in painting,' even were
all the skill of mind and deftness of hand of

the people of Wu to be exhausted, still could not surpass the style and taste to be found within the walls of the Wen family. I once visited you, and saw for myself how elegance was expressed in the architecture of halls and beauty in the architecture of pavilions, it was beyond the power of man to describe, but this work of compilation is engirdled within you, your brush relentlessly consumes paper, is this not too much?" Wen Zhenheng replied, "Not so, my fear is that as time passes and, as you said, the people of Wu change in mind and artistry, then the knowledge of the source of these leisured pursuits and superfluous things will be lost to later generations. I make this compilation as a precaution against that." True indeed! The phrase "excise the elaborate, expel the extravagant" could well suffice as a foreword to this book. I shall proclaim it to the world, so that all should read this book and sense both the taste, talent and sensibility of Wen Zhenheng and the depth of his purpose as well.

Shen Chunze

Fig. 19 *Making Tea in the Forest* (detail)
Wen Zhengming
Ink and color on paper
Height 84.1 cm × Width 26.4 cm
Palace Museum, Taibei

An eminent scholar sits at ease in the shade of a great tree making tea and savoring its fragrance, a classic example of the elegant scholar taking tea. Wen Zhengming was an outstanding Ming dynasty literary figure, calligrapher and artist.

CHAPTER ONE
STUDIOS AND RETREATS

It is best to live amongst hills and water, next best in a village and after that on the outskirts of a town. Those of my generation who cannot follow in the footsteps of the early Han dynasty (206 BC–AD 220) hermits Wu Shi and Tang Bing and dwell amidst crags and ravines and must exist amidst the bustle of market noise, need have our gates and courts fresh and elegant, our studios and retreats quiet and peaceful, our pavilions broad and spacious in spirit and our studies filled with an atmosphere of remote tranquility. They should be planted with various kinds of fine wood and curious bamboo and display precious objects, pictures and calligraphy so that those who dwell there forget age, those who visit forget parting and those who wander there forget weariness. When all burgeons at the end of the summer heat, the wind should sough amongst the trees bringing coolness and in the bitter cold it should be warm and comfortable. Mere extravagance of material in building and color in decorating will only serve to create a cage.

Fig. 20 *Solitary Fishing Hut by a Stream* (detail)
Tang Yin (1470–1523)
Ink and color on silk
Height 30 cm × Length 610 cm
Palace Museum, Taibei

One of the ideal lifestyles of the Ming scholar was to live in a hut in the hills. Although the thatched hut in the picture is simple, it is built overlooking water with a breeze from all quarters. It seems an abode of the immortals, the very place to live in seclusion.

Gates

The wooden crosspiece of the doorframe should have a strip of speckled bamboo (*Phyllostachys bambusoides f. tanakae*) nailed horizontally or slanting across it, either two or four strips, never six. Wooden boards on either side may be used to display carved spring couplets, following one's taste and drawn from the best of Tang poems. Where there is a stone doorsill, then the doors must be of wood. The stone should be thick and square with no hint of vulgarity. Circular door knocker plates bearing bronze butterflies or the faces of beasts or pheasants or *taotie* (an ancient Chinese mythological beast with a reputation for greed) (fig. 21) may be nailed to the door, otherwise copper or finely worked iron cast in the old-fashioned way may be used. Brass and cupronickel may not be used. With lacquer, the only colors may be vermilion, purple and black, no other.

Steps

May consist of three to ten steps, the higher the more antique, they should be cut from veined stone and planted with several stems of dwarf lily turf (*Ophiopogon japonicum*) or ornamental grass that spread and overhang the side of the steps. Steps formed from layers of water-patterned Taihu stone are known as "rough waves." This construction is wonderful indeed but not easy to achieve. The inner part of the chamber should be higher than the outer and tessellated with undressed moss-stained stone. Only then will it have the feeling of a mountain valley.

Windows

Wood should be used for the window frame into which should be inserted a fine lattice containing three apertures or eyes no more than two *cun* (roughly 6 cm) square. A wooden sill of one *chi* (roughly 32 cm) may be added beneath the window. In buildings devoted to

Fig. 21   Pale Yellow Tripod (*Ding*) Incised with an Animal Face Pattern
Ming dynasty
Height 16.8 cm, diameter at lip 13.3 cm
Palace Museum, Taibei

The animal face pattern was mainly current during the Shang dynasty (1600–1046 BC) and early Western Zhou (1046–771 BC) periods. Believed to be endowed with the properties of exorcising evil spirits and demonstrating power, it often appeared as a decoration on entrance gates during the Warring States period (475–221 BC) and later. The rim of the tripod is decorated with two upright lugs whilst the base is joined by three columnar feet, the whole is glazed a pale yellow. The body is decorated with animal faces front and rear, which exaggerate the *taotie* pattern into an even greater display of the grandeur of this vessel.

Buddha and chambers used for Zen, the lattices are of a diamond shaped pattern or the shape of an elephant eye. A window may not consist of six leaves, but two, three or four may be used according to taste. Where the room is high, a horizontal window may be used supported by a low balustrade. Windows may have inserts of translucent shell for light or be pasted over with paper. Neither plain cotton nor silk printed with a plum blossom pattern may be used. During the months of winter for the sake of sunshine, large lattice storm shutters of a width of one *chi* (roughly 32 cm) may be fitted with vertical cording that will prevent the window paper being blown in by wind and snow. This style is very elegant and may be used in small studios and rooms. Gold lacquer may be used or the two colors vermilion and black. Neither carved patterns nor many-colored lacquers may be used (fig. 22).

Fig. 22 Windows in the Humble Administrator's Garden, Suzhou

There are many designs for window frames, in straight and curved geometrical patterns as well as those carved with flowers and animals. They are one of the most elaborate aspects of the gardens of the Jiangnan area.

Balustrades and Railings

Balustrades of stone are the most antique, though mostly used in Daoist and Buddhist temples and family graves. They may also be used along the edge of pools. Most elegant of all are two stone pillars carved with lotus flowers at two ends with wooden balustrades between. The pillars should not be too high nor can they be carved with the shapes of birds and beasts. Vermilion railings and railings in the form of a swan's neck backrest bench may be used in pavilions, waterside pavilions (*xie*) (fig. 23), external corridors and rooms. The main hall should have great pillars of wood carved like a stone pillar with empty space between the pillars. The pillar tops should be ornamented with a persimmon decoration and the pillar painted vermilion with a

pattern of vases amidst lotus leaves in green. The swastika pattern is more suitable to the chambers of ladies and is not particularly refined. Subjects from pictures may be used according to taste. Railings formed from three wooden crosspieces are the simplest and most convenient but are too plain and should not be used over much. There should be one panel to a pillar and no wooden upright in-between dividing it into two or three panels. In a studio or study there is no need for this.

Fig. 23 Backrests for Beauties at the Waterside Pavilion in the Suzhou classical garden

The four sides of the hibiscus waterside pavilion are equipped with backrest benches where people may take their ease.

Screen Doors①

Screen doors made from *Phoebe Zhennan* are particularly fine. Alternatively, plainly painted white, or gold painted screens are acceptable. Screen doors with scenes painted in purple or green or dappled lacquer are completely unacceptable. Nor may screen doors of six panels be used though wide ones may be used in a hall but in a study or studio a screen door may only be used by the central pillar. It is vulgar to use windows with muslin inserts or a finely latticed partition.

① Screen doors: In the Ming and Qing dynasties it was the practice in the building of halls, pavilions and studios to use door screens, window frames or wooden planking to fill in the empty wall at the rear of outer rooms.

Halls

Halls should be spacious and imposing in their ordering. To front and rear there should be courtyards and open pavilions of several stories containing promenades that can accommodate

Fig. 24   The Hall of Distant Fragrance in the Humble Administrator's Garden (1736–1795)

The Hall of Distant Fragrance is an "open sided pavilion" and the major structure of the garden erected in the Qianlong reign. Built to face the water it has a width of three bays. In summer the scent of the lotus flowers drifts from the pool and the hall is the best place to enjoy it.

a banquet table. The four walls are best made from fine brick or otherwise painted white. The roof beams should be arched and balanced as to height and width. Steps should be made from veined stone and in a small hall there is no need for window bars (fig. 24).

Mountain Retreats

Mountain retreats must be bright and clean and not too open. Light and cleanliness lift the heart but too much openness is hard on the eyes. Window bars may be fitted beneath the eaves and entrance may be gained through a veranda but all must suit the lie of the land. The central court must be sufficiently

Fig. 25 *Studio in the Woods* (detail)
Zhao Mengyu (Yuan dynasty, 1279–1368)
Ink and color on paper
Height 102.4 cm × Width 51.3 cm
Palace Museum, Taibei

In a scene of the utmost refinement, a scholar sits cross-legged in a simple mountain studio beneath a bare tree in a wood. Clumps of narcissus can be seen beneath the tree.

people plant a climbing fig (*Ficus pumila*) at its foot and splash the wall with fermented fish innards to encourage it to climb; this may appear elegant but is not as fine as a plain white wall (fig. 25).

Inner Rooms or Cells

Suitable for cold nights in the depths of winter, they should follow the construction of the warm rooms of the north and may be furnished with a sleeping couch and Zen chair. The courtyard in front should be broad so as to receive the sunlight and there should be a west window for the setting sun. There is no need for a north window.

large to plant flowers and trees and display *penjing* (bonsai). During the summer, the north door may be removed to allow the flow of air between the front and back. The borders of the court should be watered with rice soup, once soaked with rain they will produce an attractive bed of green moss. Peacock moss (*Selaginella uncinata*) should be planted amongst the surrounding brickwork, which having spread then burgeons into a luxuriant green. The front wall should be suitably low and some

Buddha Halls

The platform should be about five *chi* (roughly 1.6 m) high and approached by a flight of steps, there should be a small open corridor in front with side doors to left and right, the space at the back to a depth of three pillars is devoted to the Buddha. The courtyard may be furnished with stones and display Buddhist banners and pennants. A separate door may lead to a small chamber at the back containing a sleeping couch.

Bridges

For large ponds and streams, bridges should be constructed from veined stone finely carved with clouds or scenery and without a hint of vulgarity. For rivulets and mountain streams bridges are best built from rocks planted about with dwarf lily turf. Plank bridges should be built with three separate sections or turns and a wooden handrail. Swastika patterns in the railing should be avoided. There are those

Fig. 26 Garden bridges delicately lie across ponds and pools to form a girdle that ties pavilions and verandas into the garden's scenery.

Fig. 27 *Tasting Tea*
Wen Zhengming
Ink and color on paper
Height 88.3 cm × Width 25.2 cm
Palace Museum, Taibei

A scholar has built a small tea hut where, when a
guest calls, they sit talking and taking tea in what may
well be termed a deep understanding of life. The
thatched hut is elegantly situated amidst trees and
running water and has gleaming tables and couches.
Within, two figures sit opposite each other tasting
tea. In the adjacent shack the stove burns brightly as
a boy servant fans the flames to boil water.

who use Taihu stone; this is vulgar. Stone
bridges should not incorporate three arches
or apertures, plank bridges should have no
right-angled turns (fig. 26) and bridges with
pavilions on top are to be avoided most of all.

Tea Huts

Build a small chamber beside a mountain
retreat and equip it with the implements for
preparing tea and make a boy responsible
for the duties of making tea and providing it
for the debates of the daylight hours and for
sitting upright in contemplation at night. This
is the principal matter of the secluded life and
is not to be cast away (fig. 27).

Fig. 28 *Clasping a* Qin *at the Edge of a Stream* (detail)
Xia Gui (Southern Song dynasty, 1127–1279)
Ink and color on paper
Height 25.5 cm × Width 26 cm
Palace Museum, Beijing

The *qin* takes pride of place amongst the four arts of playing the *qin*, chess, calligraphy and painting. From time immemorial, hermits and men of ability have excelled at playing the *qin*. To play on the *qin* beneath the moon symbolizes the ultimate elegance of the leisured life.

A Pavilion in Which to Play the *Qin*

In the pavilion in which they played the *qin* the ancients often buried a large jar in which a bronze bell was suspended that resonated with the sound of the *qin*. It is better still to play at the bottom of a building where the board ceiling prevents the sound from dispersing and concentrates it in the broad space below so that the music sounds strongly. For greater elegance the pavilion may also be situated amongst pine trees or bamboo, amidst crags and caves, below a hut of stone set amid scenery of purity and tranquility (fig. 28).

Bathhouses

Bathhouses comprise two chambers separated by a wall, the front chamber has an iron vessel installed and the rear contains fuel in readiness. It particularly needs to be a private chamber impervious to wind and cold. A well should be dug close to the wall equipped with a windlass for drawing water to be carried in through the wall. There should be a drain at the back to carry away the water. Implements for taking a bath and towels should be included.

Paths and Courtyards

For the best appearance paths and large courtyards should be paved with Wukang stone from Zhejiang. Where rocks are used amongst flowers and at the edge of water, or tile shards are piled in an incline, over time, rain will produce moss that will create an air of natural antiquity. Is it really necessary to expend vast sums on building before a place may be considered to be of scenic renown (fig. 29)?

Buildings

Buildings used for sleeping should be distantly secluded; those designed for gazing abroad should be open and imposing; those intended for the storage of books and paintings should be bright and dry, tall and capacious. This is the grand principle of building. A building (*lou*) has windows on all four sides, those at the front open, those at the rear and the two

Fig. 29 Flower-Patterned Paving in the Humble Administrator's Garden

sides shuttered. A building (*ge*) is square, each side the same. There may be neither terrace nor awning in front and the floor may not be paved with brick. Since they are called *lou* and *ge* respectively, each must have its ordained form, if it is paved with brick, where is the difference with a building of a single story? A building of three stories is extremely vulgar. If the ground floor pillars are slightly taller, then a flat roof may be installed above.

Terraces

In the building of terraces (fig. 30) six cornered terraces are to be avoided, the construction should be determined according to the characteristics of the ground. If the terrace is built on a mound an appearance of elegance may be achieved by the addition of vermilion railings of rough wood.

There is further appeal in the paving of Chinese gardens where creativity of design far outstrips extravagance of expenditure in importance. The paving of paths with colored pebbles and stone shards, together with the variety of design, bears many meanings whilst at the same time physically separating and organizing space.

Fig. 30 *Walking Beneath the Moon on the Jade Terrace* (detail)

Anon. (Song dynasty, 960–1279)
Ink and color on silk
Height 25.6 cm × Width 26.7 cm
Palace Museum, Beijing

This picture shows four ladies of court enjoying the sight of the moon at the Mid-Autumn Festival. At the same time it also accurately depicts part of the architectural feature known as a *tai*—terrace with its railings and the head of its lotus flower-topped columns decorated with lamps.

Summary

A "dust catcher," commonly known as a "heavenly flower board" or ceiling, may not be used; it can only be used in official premises. Floors may be used in rooms. Bamboo mats may not be used in heated rooms. Woolen rugs may be used as a floor covering but nothing equals the elegance of fine brick. In the dampness of the south, paving may be laid on supports above the ground; this is worth a little extra expense. Rooms may not have five pillars or two side rooms. Front and rear halls may not be laid out in the form of the character *gong* (工), this too closely resembles official premises, though it may be used for retiring rooms. There must always be women and servants' side passages to main rooms. Courtyards should be built slightly east of rooms to diminish the heat of the western sun; they should not be long and narrow or short and broad. Pavilions (*ting*) should not be pointed at the top and narrow at the bottom, nor small hexagons, nor should the roof resemble a gourd, nor should they be roofed with thatch, they must not look like bell towers or city wall watchtowers. Stairs should ascend at the rear and should not be placed at either side. Bricks laid in a twisting pattern are most elegant. Waterside pavilions and gazebos at the edge of water may use curtains of blue silk as shade from the sun and purple silk as a screen from snow and wind but no other. The use of ordinary cloth such as that on pleasure boats and market medicine stalls is to be most avoided. Small rooms should not be partitioned in the middle, if there is a north window, they should be made into two separate rooms. Paper may not be used for walls nor should rooms appear as bare as a hole in a rock; that would be no different to a bathhouse, beloved by the vulgar, difficult to believe though it is. Planks should not be added alongside windows with a swastika pattern lattice. Colored flower-and-bird paintings should not be painted in the corners of rooms. The ancients set much store by inscriptions on walls and even if Gu Kaizhi (c. 345–409) of the Eastern Jin dynasty and Lu Tanwei (?–c. 485) of the Southern dynasties (420–589) were to paint landscapes, or Zhong Yao (151–230) of the Three Kingdoms and Wang Xizhi (321–379) of the Eastern Jin dynasty were to add calligraphy, it could not be better than a plain wall. Long corridors should not all be the same and should be changed in layout so that vulgarity is to be avoided. Screens and fences of bamboo are not to be used, nor may brass or cupronickel be used for door hinges. The borders of courtyards may not be paved with square bricks though

Fig. 31 *Chiwen* Roof Ridge Decoration at the Tiantai Temple, Pingshun County, Changzhi, Shanxi Province

The *chiwen* is an ancient Chinese mythological beast, one of the nine sons of the dragon, in form like a four-footed snake with its tail cut off. It is also a frequently seen decoration on the roof ridge ends of ancient Chinese buildings. Placing a pair of *chiwen* facing each other from either end of a roof ridge signifies a prayer for protection from fire.

they may be used
on flat roof terraces.
Ornamental brackets
should not be used between
the crossbeams between two pillars and the
roof ridge, this is old-fashioned and rather
inelegant. Partitions should not be of planking
but of brick. Twisting patterns may not
be painted on roof beams, nor patterns of
interlocking lozenges in gold. If because of
the age of the building the paintwork has also
aged and redecoration is unavoidable it must
be done by a master craftsman. All approaches
to entrances should be slightly curved and not
too direct. Halls should have three pillars and
a side room in which a sleeping couch may be
placed. The courtyard on the north should
not be too large on account of the bitter
north wind. There should be no railings in
the center of the room as in the form of the
present-day alcove bedstead or roofed bed
chamber. Holes should not be made in walls
to take a wardrobe and pottery tiles should
not be used for courtyard walls. There are also
those who manufacture pottery tiles in the
shape of copper cash or plum blossom; all this
should be struck down. There are also *chiwen*
roof ridge ends (representing the ninth son of
the mythological dragon that looks east and
west and swallows fire), placed at the two ends
of roof ridges as protection against fire and
known from antiquity, though it is unknown
what those in use today are supposed to
resemble (fig. 31). These should be made
in the ancient fashion or otherwise follow
the form to be found on buildings and in
paintings. Tiles beneath the eaves may not be
whitewashed and for the utmost elegance large
split palm leaves should be used to carry away
rainwater, otherwise bamboo may be used but
not wood or tin. There should be no open-
sided matsheds. These are erected in official
premises for the hearing of litigants. How
they are used in ordinary homes is not known.
Plum blossom-patterned windows may not be
used. For hanging screens or curtains within a

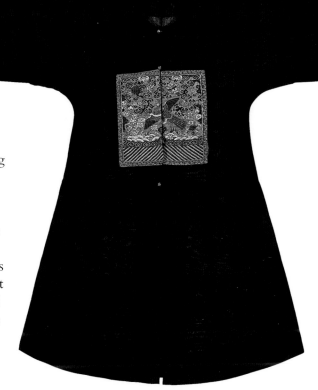

Fig. 32   Historical Official Uniform

The official uniform of civil and military officials
in ancient China very distinctly reflects the graded
hierarchy of the time. Differences in official rank
were denoted by differences in the design of the
embroidered panel on the garment, for example, red-
crowned crane, peacock, *qilin* and lion.

hall, speckled bamboo
from Wenzhou is the
best; patterns like
birds and animals
may not be placed on
hangings or curtains
like *buzi*① (fig. 32),
nor may such characters as Hill of Longevity
(*shoushan*) or Sea of Prosperity (*fuhai*). In
sum, suit the form to the place, each place
possesses that which suits it, be ancient rather
than fashionable, be simple rather than merely
clever, be restrained rather than vulgarly
ostentatious. As to the ideals of purity and
elegance, they are innate, born of one's inner
self, and are not to be lightly spoken of by
those who must always have an explanation
for everything.

① *Buzi*: Under the
Ming system, badges
of the nine civil and
military ranks were
embroidered on panels
that were stitched to
the front and back of
official dress.

CHAPTER TWO
FLOWERS AND TREES

One tends flowers for a year to see them for only ten days; hence the need to shade them from the sun with screens and protect them with bells to scare the birds away. It is not just a question of a splendid appearance. The planting of flowers and trees should be reckoned by the *mu* (the *mu* is equivalent to 667 square meters). As to the edges of courtyards and balustrades, they should be filled with an exuberance of twisted branches and ancient trees of rare varieties and exotic names, spread in profusion, both scattered and close. They may grow aslant amongst the stones at the water's edge or appear as a forest, or stand in isolated splendor. Plants should not be overdone but planted according to the place and the changing seasons as if in a picture. Peach and pear may not be grown in a courtyard and are best viewed from afar, red plum blossoms and purple peach blossoms are planted as an adornment amongst other trees and should not be over-planted. The plum blossom grows in the hills. Those that have moss on them may be moved to a flower fence or trellis where they will appear the most ancient. The flower of the apricot

does not blossom for long and opens at a time of wind and rain and can only be enjoyed for a while. No winter can be without wintersweet. Other things such as bean frames and vegetable patches, having rather the flavor of a mountain dwelling and although not bad in themselves, should be removed to a separate tilled place of several *qing* (one *qing* is equal to about six hectares). It would not be good taste for them to be in a courtyard, more so for stone blocks and wooden posts used for building frames and trellises. That would be even worse. As to the cultivation of orchids and chrysanthemums, in ancient times there were methods for each. These should be drawn upon for the instruction of gardeners and an examination of these skills and arts is also the task of the elegantly secluded gentleman.

Fig. 33 "The Fourth Month" from *Weather of the Twelve Months* (detail)

Anon. (Qing dynasty)
Ink and color on Silk
Height 175 cm × Width 97 cm
Palace Museum, Taibei

The complete series of *Weather of the Twelve Months* is a descriptive representation of the ordinary life of each month of the year, not only of people in general but also of the interests and intellectual tastes of the gentleman scholar of traditional society. In this depiction of the fourth month, trees are gradually coming into leaf, flowers blossom and people take their leisure gazing at the flowers under a rain-darkened sky.

Fig. 34 *Birds and Flowers* (detail)
Qian Xuan (c. 1239–c. 1300)
Ink and color on paper
Height 38 cm × Length 316.7 cm
Tianjin Museum

Under the hand of the artist two pale pink tree peonies blossom amongst green leaves that droop slightly to the left as if a sudden breeze has just brushed past. The color is delicate and the style refined.

Tree Peony and Herbaceous Peony

The tree peony (*Paeonia suffruticosa*) is the king of flowers and the herbaceous peony (*Paeonia lactiflora*) is his minister; they are the nobility of flowers. There can be nothing poverty-stricken in their cultivation and appreciation. Using veined stone as a railing, plant them irregularly but in order. At a banquet when they flower, support them with a wooden frame. Spread a green oilcloth above to protect them from sunlight and in the evening and at night hang lamps and candles to illuminate them. Do not arrange them together in rows or put them in wooden tubs or earthenware pots (figs. 34, 35).

Fig. 35 Herbaceous Peony

Magnolia

Magnolias (*Magnolia denudata*) may be planted in front of formal buildings. They may be arranged in groups and when they flower it is like a vision of pure white, a garden of elegant jade, worthy of being called superb (fig. 36). There is another purple kind called *mubi* (*Magnolia liliflora*) that cannot bear to be handmaid to the magnolia,

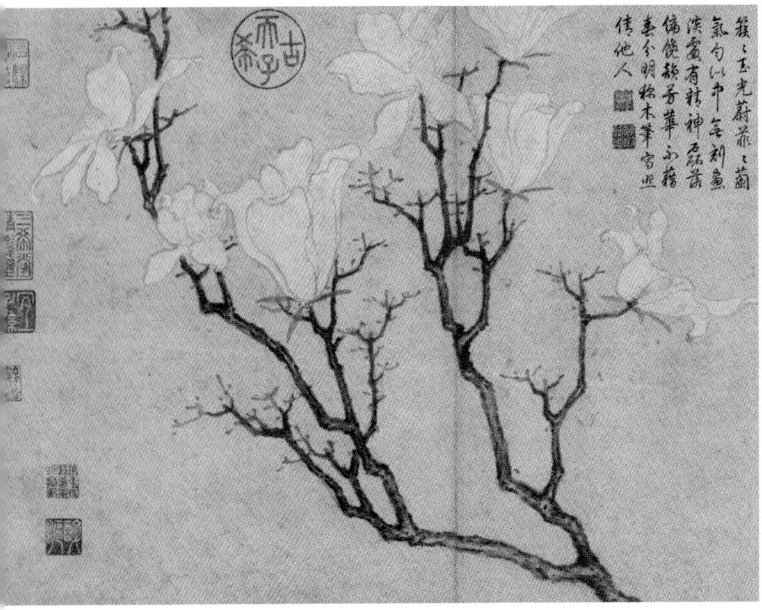

Fig. 36 "Magnolias" from *Album of Paintings from Life*
Shen Zhou
Ink and color on paper
Height 34.8 cm × Width 56.5 cm
Palace Museum, Taibei

Magnolias were often planted in the courtyards of houses as a symbol of the "riches and honor of a jade hall." In this picture, the background is shaded in a pale blue-green that uses the technique of *liubai*, leaving blank—dynamic emptiness, to emphasize the pure white of the flowers and give an effect of quiet elegance.

Container
Height 25 cm, diameter at mouth 2.7 cm, base diameters 10.2 × 2.7 cm
Ming dynasty, Yongle period (1403–1424)
Palace Museum, Taibei

The flask has a narrow mouth, a slender neck and an oblate belly. The base is flat and there are no feet. The whole carries a blue-and-white decoration with a blossoming camellia on the belly.

and was called *xinyi* by the ancients. However, the magnolias named after the *xinyiwu* and *mulanchai* vistas at the Tang dynasty poet Wang Wei's country villa at Wangchuan (in present day Lantian county, Shaanxi Province) are not the same plant under different names but two varieties.

Crab Apple

The crab apples of Changzhou (in the south east of the present-day Sichuan basin) are sweet but are now no longer to be had; next are those from Xifu (*Malus micromalus*), next *Chaenomeles lagenaria* and then *Malus halliana*. I consider the *Malus halliana* sweetly tender like Yang Guifei (719–756) when intoxicated, and better than *Malus micromaus* and *Chaenomeles lagenaria*. The quince (*Chaenomeles sinensis*) is like a crab apple, which is why there are crab apple quinces. However, the quince flowers first and then comes into leaf whereas the crab apple is the other way round. That is the difference between the two. There is another kind called begonia (*Begonia evansiana*), which prefers damp shade and is suitable for planting by shaded steps. Of all autumn flowers this is the most splendid and may be planted in large numbers.

Camellia

The camellias of Sichuan (*Camellia japonica*) and of Yunnan (*Camellia reticulata*) are precious, the yellow ones are particularly difficult to obtain. The common people mostly plant them to accompany magnolias as they flower at the same time. Their colors of red and white are magnificent but they are a little vulgar. There is another variety called Drunken Guifei (*Camellia japonica var. anemoniflora*) that flowers in the snow and is even more attractive (fig. 37).

Peach

Peach trees (*Prunus persica*) are magical and can bring demons under control, they may be planted in groves, as if entering the fairy peach garden of Wuling, they have their own splendor but should not be planted in pots and have no place in a courtyard. By their nature they fruit early and wither after ten years, thus they are called "short lived flowers." The jade peach (*Prunus persica var. duplex*) (fig. 38) and the flowering peach (*Prunus persica var. dianthiflora*) flower a little later but are more beautiful than ordinary peach trees. They may be planted in numbers at the edge of ponds. It is vulgar to place peach trees and willows together.

Fig. 38 Jade Peach

Chinese Plum

A peach blossom is like a beautiful woman singing and dancing and must be planted in quantities. The Chinese plum (*Prunus salicina*) is like a woman Daoist, suited to the hazy mist of rocks and springs but not in great quantities (fig. 39). There is another kind known as *Prunus japonica*, which is more beautiful still.

Apricot

Together with the red Chinese plum and the flat peach (*Prunus persica var. platycarpa*) it is as if the apricot (*Prunus armeniaca*) forms one of the three legs of an ancient ceremonial tripod. Its flowers are charming (fig. 40) and together with the others may be grown on a terrace in groups of ten.

Fig. 40   Apricot Blossom

Plum Blossom

The man of elegant remoteness has flowers as his companions and is especially partial to the plum blossom (*Prunus mume*) (fig. 41). One may transplant those protected by moss and sealed in lichen and with branches of slightly ancient appearance to grow amongst rocks and in courtyard borders. This is most elegantly antique. Plant several *mu* of them and when they flower, sit or recline in their midst; this will raise the spirits and settle the mind. The most splendid is *Prunus mume var. viridicalyx* though the red plum blossom (*Prunus mume var. alphandii*) is rather vulgar; moreover there are those with stems twisted like the horns of a young dragon that go in pots and are curious

Fig. 39   *Silk Tapestry Chinese Plum*
Silk
Height 48.3 cm × Width 45.6 cm
Palace Museum, Taibei

This silk tapestry (*kesi*) is studded with white blossoms. A single butterfly dances lightly amongst the blossoms and every thread exudes a sense of spring.

Fig. 41   *A Solitary Bird amongst Plum Blossom*
Bian Wenjin (c. 1356–c. 1428)
Ink and color on silk
Height 24.7 cm × Width 23.8 cm
Palace Museum, Taibei

A bird perches amongst the white plum blossom, its head raised as it gazes into the distance. The technique is finely detailed and the application of color is simple yet elegant.

Fig. 42 *White Rambler Rose* (detail)
Ma Yuan (Southern Song dynasty)
Ink and color on silk
Height 26.2 cm × Width 25.8 cm
Palace Museum, Beijing

A white rambler rose, meticulously represented with massive blooms and luxuriant foliage, projects both vitality and elegance of style.

in the extreme. The best of the wintersweet (*Chimonanthus praecox*) is *Chimonanthus praecox var. grandiflorus*; the *Chimonanthus praecox var. concolor* is next and the *Chimonanthus praecox var. intermedius* is the least, but in the months of cold, courtyards cannot be without them.

Winter Daphne (*Daphne odora*)

Legend has it that a Buddhist monk once fell into a noonday sleep on Lushan Mountain (in present day Jiujiang city of Jiangxi Province) and dreamed that he smelled the fragrance of flowers. He awoke and found the flower,

Fig. 43 Winter Daphne

hence its name "sleep's fragrance." Those around were amazed and pronounced it "an auspicious sign amidst the flowers" hence the name *ruixiang* (fig. 43). There is another kind named golden border (*Daphne odora var. marginata*), which is particularly valued. It is thick stemmed and has an intense fragrance that seems to absorb the scent of other plants for its own use. It is thus called a plant robber; this is no empty belief.

Rambler Rose (*Rosa multiflora*) and Wood Perfume (*Muxiang—Rosa banksiae*)

In the garden vistas of other people, I have in the past seen screens made from bamboo intertwined with rambler roses (fig. 42) of five colors①. A tall trellis of *muxiang* (*Rosa banksiae*) is known as a "*muxiang* awning." When everybody sits beneath it as they flower, how does it differ from a market food stall? Furthermore, the two kinds cannot grow unless supported by a frame. At a pinch they may be moved to the women's quarters where they may be picked by the ladies. There is another kind called yellow rambler (*Rosa hugonis*), the most precious of all, brightly colored and pleasing to the eye. Even more grow profusely in the wild and are known as "wild ramblers" (*Rosa multiflora*), with a heavier fragrance and may be compared with the rose (*Rosa rugosa*). Others such as "precious visage" (*baoxiang*), "golden sand" (*jinshaluo*), "golden bowl" (*jinboyu*)②, "Buddha's smile" (*Rubus rosifolius var. coronarius*), "seven sisters" (*Rosa cathayensis var. platyphylla*), "ten sisters" (cultivar of *Rosa cathayensis*), "spiny briar" (*Rosa roxburghii*) and Chinese rose (*Rosa chinensis*) are all more or less similar in appearance and cultivation.

① "Rambler roses of five colors": an abundance of small flowers, five or six to a stem, divided by color into deep and pale red.

② The botanical names for *baoxiang*, *jinshaluo*, and *jinboyu* remain unclarified.

Fig. 44   Chinese Redbud

Rose

The rose (*Rosa rugosa*), also called the "hesitant flower" has an overpowering fragrance and may be used in a pomander though this is not something suitable to persons of elegant

Fig. 45   *Rosa rugosa*

seclusion. The tender stems are covered in spines and it is not a refined sight, the color of the flower is rather vulgar and it does not make a suitable ornament in hair or belt though it may be used in food. In the land of Wu there are many *mu* under cultivation from which rich profits are made (fig. 45).

Chinese Redbud and Kerria

The redbud (*Cercis chinensis*) has bare branches and flowers that resemble earrings of jade (fig. 44). In shape, color and fragrance it is nothing outstanding. It has only achieved prominence because of the Han dynasty story of the three brothers who divided their fortune; they returned to harmony after the redbud in the courtyard withered on hearing it was to be split amongst them but sprang back into life when it was reprieved. In my view it would be better to plant more kerria (*Kerria japonica*) for a better understanding of the poet's meaning (fig. 46).

Crape Myrtle

There are four kinds of crape myrtle (*Lagerstroemia indica*): apart from the purple kind the white one is called *baiwei* [*L. indica* Linn. f. *alba* (Nichols.) Rehd.], the red is called *hongwei* and the purple and blue one is called *cuiwei*. This flower blossoms from the fourth month to the ninth month and is commonly

Fig. 46   Kerria

called the "hundred days of red." It is planted in hill gardens and is called "friend forever." It is best viewed at a distance. In the north, it is called the monkey tree because it has no bark and monkeys are thereby deprived of their agility. This is a curious name.

Pomegranate

Fig. 47   Pomegranate Blossom

The flower of the pomegranate (*Punica granatum*) is greater than its fruit. There are three kinds; large red, peach red and pale white. The many-leaved one called *bingziliu* is as fierce as fire and seedless. It is suitable for growing at the edges of a courtyard (fig. 47).

Cotton Rosemallow

This cotton rosemallow (*Hibiscus mutabilis*) may be planted on the banks of ponds, at best overlooking the water. It would be tasteless to plant them elsewhere. There are those who "dip" the flower stamens into indigo dye

and then wrap the flower tip in the paper so that when it opens it is blue-green in color. They believe this to be splendid; it is utterly unspeakable (fig. 48).

Champaka (*Magnolia champaca*)

Called "*Yue* peach" and "forest magnolia" and commonly known as *zhizi* (gardenia) it was anciently known as "the friend of Zen." It comes from the Western Regions[①] and is suitable for planting in buildings dedicated to Buddha. It should not be sniffed closely as it harbors a minute insect that enters the human nostril. It should not be planted in rooms.

① Western Regions: from the Han dynasty onwards the term referred to the states that lay to the west of Dunhuang.

Jasmine, Royal Jasmine (*Jasminum grandiflorum*), Magnolia Coco

Jasmine (*Jasminum sambac*) may be most widely distributed on summer nights when rooms will be filled with its fragrance at the puff of the wind wheel (fig. 49). In Zhangjiang (the Gan River area in present day Jiangxi Province) it is woven into fences. When it is in

Fig. 48 "Cotton Rosemallow" from *An Album of Plants and Flowers*
Sun Kehong (1532–1611)
Ink and color on paper
Height 15 cm × Width 46.5 cm (folding fan format)
Palace Museum, Taibei

In this elegantly colored and captivating fan leaf, several cotton rosemallow blossoms droop gently downwards and a reed extends to one side.

flower thousands of boats assemble at Huqu (the northern outskirts of present day Suzhou in Jiangsu Province), hence the reason that its flower market prospers in the early summer. When cultivated appropriately it will flower annually, however, the profusion of flowers and leaves does not make it suitable for low tables but unlike the magnolia coco it may be put in vases (fig. 50).

Azalea

The azalea (*Rhododendron*) has vividly colored flowers. It is shade-loving by nature and abhors the heat. It may be planted beneath trees in the shade. When in flower it may be placed on low tables. There is another kind called "Bright Hill Red" (*Rhododendron simsii*), which may be planted amongst rocks and is also known as "Goat's Trample" (fig. 51).

Fig. 49 Jasmine

Fig. 50 Royal Jasmine

Fig. 51 Azalea

Fig. 52   *A Scholar's Window on the Pines*
Wang Meng
Ink and color on paper
Height 107.4 cm × Width 32.6 cm
Palace Museum, Taibei

Several simple, unassuming studio huts stand beneath some tall pine trees. A scholar sits in contemplation on the riverbank. This is an archetypal scene from the life of a literary gentleman.

Pine

Although pine (*Pinus*) and cedar are spoken of in the same breath and are the noblest of all, pride of place must go to the pine. The *huangshan* pine (*Pinus taiwanensis*) from Tianmu Mountain (of Lin'an in present day Zhejiang Province) is the best but it is not easy to plant. The *guazi* pine (*Pinus bungeana*) may be planted in front of halls, in wide courtyards or on terraces and there is no reason why they may not be planted opposite each other. A single pine may be planted outside a studio with a platform of veined stone beneath or with a balustrade of Taihu stone (fig. 52) and narcissus, orchids (*Cymbidium*) and daylilies (*Hemerocallis fulva*) may be scattered beneath them. The horsetail pine may be planted on earth mounds and with its dragon scale bark and the sighing of the wind in its branches how can it not stand comparison with the majesty of the Five Pines[1] and Nine Li[2].

① Five Pines: according to legend the emperor Qin Shihuang (259–210 BC) was caught in a sudden rainstorm when ascending Mount Taishan and had to shelter beneath a group of five pine trees that he subsequently appointed "the five officials."

② Nine Li: a reference to Nine Li Pines on the Western Lake planted by the Tang dynasty official Yuan Renjing (dates unknown) when he was in charge of Hangzhou. The pines were planted to left and right in three rows of verdant green. The place became known as Nine Li Pines.

Hibiscus (*Hibiscus syriacus*)

The lowliest of the plants (fig. 53), known in ancient times as *shunhua* "disappearing in the blink of an eye," a name from the most distant past, it is also called *zhaojun* "short lived." There is no reason why they may

Fig. 53 Hibiscus (*Mujin—Hibiscus syriacus*)

not be planted amongst fences or by stream banks in the wild but I cannot approve of those who insist upon calling it a great friend of the garden.

Osmanthus

When a stand of osmanthus (*Osmanthus fragrans*) flowers it may truly be called "the cavern and seat of fragrance." Two *mu* of land (roughly 1334 m²) may be cleared and all kinds planted there with a pavilion amongst them, but other trees may not be scattered with them and they cannot be labeled with such phrases as "heavenly fragrance" and "small hill." The ground beneath the trees should be as flat as the palm of your hand and should not be spat upon, so that when the blossom falls to the ground it may be gathered up and used for food.

Willow

Trees that have leaves that point upwards are *Salix gracilistyla* and those whose leaves hang down are *Salix babylonica*, weeping willows, which need to be planted overlooking streams or ponds. Its tender leaves, green and yellow, brush the waters in carefree leisure (fig. 54). Moreover, it does not harbor

Fig. 54 "Solitary Fisherman by the Willow Pool" from the Album *A Thatched Pavilion Amongst Streams and Hills*
Attributed to Shen Zhou
Ink and color on paper
Height 28 cm × Width 43.5 cm
Palace Museum, Taibei

A solitary scholar sits in a pavilion fishing in a pool bordered by willow trees whose fronds brush the water— a scene of deep satisfaction.

insects, which makes it even more estimable. The *Tamarix chinensis* are splendid as well and have a certain feminine quality. The poplar and wingnut (*Pterocarya stenoptera*) do not merit inclusion.

Boxwood

Whilst boxwood (*Buxus sinica*) may not actually shrink in a leap year it certainly grows with difficulty. The best for appreciation are those over one *zhang* (about three meters) in height with green leaves but it is not suitable for growing in pots.

Chinese Scholar Tree (*Sophora japonica*), Elm (*Ulmus*)

These trees may be planted in a courtyard where they can shade a doorway just like a jade-green canopy. The scholar tree has naturally bent drooping branches and branch and leaves hang like a mist. The one called *Sophora japonica var. pendula* is also worthy of viewing. The others, for example Chinese photinia (*Photinia serrulata*), Chinese privet (*Ligustrum lucidum*), firs (*Cunninghamia lanceolata*) and cypress are trees of the tomb and not suitable for gardens.

Fig. 55 *Dreaming in the Shade of a Parasol Tree* (detail)
Tang Yin
Ink on paper
Height 62 cm × Width 30.9 cm
Palace Museum, Beijing

In this black and white treatment of his subject, the artist depicts a figure sitting in a folding chair in the shade of a parasol tree with his face raised and eyes closed, his expression vividly represented. In the accompanying poem the artist explains that the picture is a portrayal of how after suffering many tribulations and setbacks he had come to see through the temptations of the mundane world, had abandoned the pursuit of fame, and had settled for a life of seclusion.

little from the *Ailanthus altissima*. The scented kind is the toona tree and the stinking kind is *Ailanthus altissima*. They may be planted in numbers by garden walls for culinary purposes (fig. 56).

Ginkgo

Fig. 56 Toona Tree—Buds and Leaves

The foliage of the ginkgo tree (*Ginkgo biloba*) is sparse and at its most attractive when freshly green. In the land of Wu it may be found in Buddhist temples and the well-known gardens of certain ancient families, where there are ginkgos of great girth. There is no need for fresh planting.

Chinese Parasol Tree

The parasol tree (*Firmiana simplex*) is good for shade and its trunk is as green as kingfisher jade. It may be planted in large courtyards (fig. 55). The day it is planted the branches should be wiped clean and pruned so that the tree resembles a picture. Do not choose those with bare branches that grow straight up without others to the side, those with leaves like a fist or parasol, or those that produce tendrils of cotton. The seeds of the tree may be used to make tea. Those that grow on hilltops are called *Aleurites montana* and their seed may be pressed to produce oil.

Candleberry Tree (*Sapium sebiferum*)

At the height of autumn the leaves are an attractive red in color and it is hardier than the Chinese sweet gum (*Liquidambar formosana*) (fig. 57). One or two in a wood would do justice to the Tang poet Du Mu's (803–853) line "Frosted leaves red with February flowers."

Toona Tree or Chinese Mahogany

The toona tree (*Toona sinensis*) towers majestically with sparse foliage. It differs

Fig. 57 Candleberry Tree

Fig. 58 *The Garden of Solitary Enjoyment*
(detail)
Qiu Ying
Ink and color on paper
Height 28 cm × Length 519.8 cm
Cleveland Museum of Art

During the Northern Song dynasty, the historian Sima Guang (1019–1086) compiled his *Record of the Garden of Solitary Enjoyment*, a description of the garden of his own residence in the capital Luoyang. The artist then painted a representation of the garden on the basis of the written description. This part of the painting shows a high terrace planted with bamboos and a seated figure quietly fishing. The painting achieves Wen Zhenheng's ideals for the planting of bamboos, though by different means.

Bamboo

Bamboo is best planted on raised mounds of earth surrounded by a stream crossed by a small bridge, where steps ascend to a terrace at the top and one may sit or lie with hair unbound as majestic as a man amongst a forest of ten thousand bamboo (fig. 58). Or one may dig several *mu* of land and, clearing the trees, surround it with a low stone base and a vermilion balustrade with stone pillars and, leaving not a speck of dust or single leaf, sit on the ground or have stone platforms or benches. The *Phyllostachys pubescens* is first amongst the bamboos with long branches and thick trunks, but they are suited to the hills rather than the city; *Phyllostachys dulcis* is best in the city. Other bamboo is not so elegant. The four kinds *Phyllostachys nigra var. kenonis, Phyllostachys viridiglaucescens, Phyllostachys bambusoides var. tanakae,* and *Phyllostachys nigra* may all do but *Phyllostachys praecox* is the worst. *Bambusa multiplex* does not merit inclusion. There are other varieties of bamboo such as *Phyllostachys nuda, Phyllostachys angusta, Indocalamus tessellatus, Chimonobambusa quadrangularis, Phyllostachys viridis f.youngii* called jasper in gold and *Bambusa multiplex var.nana* called phoenix tail. Bamboo should not be planted as part of a flowered fence nor in a level courtyard but several stems may be planted upright along a stretch of wall. Thickets of smaller bamboos such as "*Xiaoxiang*

bamboo"① are suitable for planting on the banks of rocky pools and present an elegantly peaceful appearance. There are four methods for planting bamboo; "scattered," "dense," "shallow" and "deep." The scattered method is described as "planting a single bamboo every three or four *chi* (about 90 to 120 cm) and clearing the soil to allow it to spread." The dense method is "planting in scattered fashion but with four or five stems to a clump thus concentrating its roots." The shallow method is "not planting very deep" and the deep method is "not planting very deep but covering with soil to assist growth." With these methods there is no bamboo that does not flourish. There are also three classes of *Rhapis humilis*: as well as *Rhapis excelsa* and short stemmed both have short stems and drooping leaves that can be grown in a pot; and also *Rhapis major*, with few nodes and hard leaves, it lacks refinement but can be used to make the spines of fans or the rollers for scrolls.

① *Xiaoxiang* bamboo: botanical name not established.

Fig. 59 *Contemplating a Chrysanthemum* (detail)
Shi Tao
Ink and color on paper
Height 99.5 cm × Width 40.2 cm
Palace Museum, Beijing

The painting depicts the interior of a courtyard adjacent to a dilapidated building where in a room with a sleeping couch a scholar sits contemplating a chrysanthemum. Outside, two boy servants are moving a pot of chrysanthemums indoors. Both the scenery beyond the courtyard and the elegant chrysanthemums in the interior increase the remoteness of the hermit's existence from the secular world by several measures of tranquility.

Chrysanthemum

When the chrysanthemum (*Dendranthema morifolium*) is at its most magnificent in the land of Wu, its acquisitive enthusiasts may take the blooms by the hundred, in all their different colors and arranging them by height, from tallest to shortest then appreciate and enjoy them in order to show off their own wealth and status. However, the true connoisseur will search out rare varieties and plant one or two in pots, with long handsome stems and rich succulent leaves, and when they blossom, place them on tables and between couches to be enjoyed whilst sitting or reclining thus achieving a sense of the true character of the flowers (fig. 59). There is a variety of chrysanthemum (*Dendranthema boreale*) from Dangkou (near Wuxi present day Jiangsu Province) with stems twisted like a parasol and flowers as dense as a satin brocade. This is very rare; one may only harvest the flowers of the other varieties of chamomile for culinary purposes. The wild chrysanthemum (*Dendranthema indicum*) may be grown in fences. The cultivation of chrysanthemums consists of "six requirements and two defenses." The requirements are: feeding and care of the shoots, suitable soil, assisting growth, rain and sunlight, pruning, and irrigation. The defenses are: defense against insects and defense against birds using the stems and leaves to build nests. These are matters for gardeners rather than people of my generation. As to using fired clay for pots or using two tiles to make a pot, it would be better to be without flowers.

Orchid

The orchids (fig. 60) from the land of Min (present day Fujian Province) are the best. Their leaves are like the point of a sword and the flowers stand taller than the leaves, just as in Qu Yuan's (c. 340–278 BC) poem *Lamentations* where he says: "In autumn the orchid stands in green and blue, with green leaves and purple stems." The next best are the orchids from Ganzhou (in present day Jiangxi Province). They are good also. No mountain studio should be without them but there should be only one pot in each place.

Any more and it will be like the flower market at Huqu. One should seek the largest old pots from the kilns of Longquan, Junzhou, and those marked *neifu* (Palace Manufactory) as well as those made by the master potter Gong Chun in Yixing. One should not use such vulgar objects as flower jars, nor vats, nor wide-mouthed ox foot pots that narrow beneath. In cultivation throughout the four seasons, in the spring when leaves and buds have already appeared and the soil in the pot is already fertile, there is no need to add fertilizer, but the leaves should be gently brushed without causing a pile of dust. In the summer, when the flower has opened and the leaves are tender, the plant should not be handled or shaken. Wait until it is in full bloom and then brush it. In the autumn, loosen the soil round the roots and water them a little with rice water, but do not smear the leaves with dirt. In the winter, place the plants indoors in a room facing the sun, however, they may be taken outside when the weather is mild. The pots should be turned frequently so that the light falls on them evenly and returned indoors in the afternoon in order to avoid damage by frost and snow. If the leaves become black and there are no flowers, it is because of too much shade. The only way to manage ants and leaf beetle is to fill a large pot or jar with water and immerse the flower pot in it and the ants will leave of their own accord. To manage leaf beetle that appears like white spots, take a basin of water and add a little sesame oil; then dip a cotton cloth in the water and wipe the leaves and they will go. These are simple methods for the cultivation of orchids. There is also an orchid called *hanglan* from Hangzhou; one called *xinglan* from the Yangxian Mountain (at Yixing, present day Jiangsu Province); and one with several flowers on a single stem called cymbidium. They may all be planted amongst rocks but need their original soil when they will flower year after year. *Chloranthus spicatus* and *Neofinetia falcata* are both kinds that are not in fashion. *Bletilla striata* has leaves like bamboo. It resembles an orchid but has no fragrance. It is a strange kind of plant. *Chloranthus spicatus* has a particularly heavy scent.

Fig. 60 *Orchids and Bamboo* (detail)
Wen Zhengming
Ink on paper
Height 26.8 cm × Length 730 cm
Palace Museum, Beijing

The orchid is one of the four gentlemen of the flower world and has always been the heart's desire of members of the literati. The leaves and flowers of the orchid are lightly depicted in ink, enough to indicate the fluency of both light and heavy in the artist's brushwork and its match with the elevated character of the orchid flower in its elegant remoteness from the commonplace.

Kui Flower

The number of kinds of *kui* flower is not determined. They are at their best in early summer when their flowers and leaves are at their most profuse and luxuriant. The kind called *rongkui* (hollyhock, *Althaea rosea*), multitudinous in appearance, may be planted in waste ground; the kind called *jinkui* (mallow, *Malva sylvestris var. mauritiana*) is as small as a coin, richly colored, enjoyable and may be planted by steps; the kind called *xiangrikui* (sunflower, *Helianthus annus*) is the least of all. The best one is called autumn *kui* (sunset hibiscus, *Abelmoschus manihot*), which flowers in the autumn. It has leaves shaped like dragons' claws and light yellow flowers.

Poppy (*Papaver somniferum*)

The best are those with petals of many forms and shapes. The kind with petals of a single leaf will produce many seeds, which are good for extracting to spice insipid dishes. No fence of herbs should be without them (fig. 61). (Editor's Note: There are many varieties of poppy and the genus includes nearly 180 species. Opium may be extracted from the opium poppy. However, in China, until the late Ming dynasty, the poppy was regarded as a flower to be enjoyed in a garden.)

Orange Daylily (*Hemerocallis fulva*)

Known as "forget sorrow" and also called "*yinan*—suitable for sons," (it was believed that if a pregnant women wore a sprig of daylily she would bear sons) it may be used in food and grows best amongst rocks and at the corners of walls. There is also a golden one that is light yellow in color and has a heavy scent. It covers the hills and valleys of Yixing (in present Jiangsu Province) but is rare in the land of Wu. Other kinds such as purple or white *Iris japonica*, *Lychnis coronata*, *Lychnis senno*, *Lycoris squamigera*, *Dianthus chinensis var. heddewigii Regel* and *Dianthus chinensis* are in a similar category of this plant.

Hosta (*Hosta plantaginea*)

In color like pure white jade and with a slight fragrance, it does well as an autumn flower. Suitable for planting by a wall, a stretch in flower looks like snow. It is extremely vulgar to plant them in pots. The purple kind is *Hosta ventricosa* and is not good.

Midday Flower (*Pentapetes phoenicea*)

It flowers at noon and falls late at night, hence it is called the midday flower. It grows to a little over one *chi* (about 30 cm) in height and may be supported on a bamboo cane so that it does not droop. It looks well if planted in stone borders.

Fig. 61 *Poppies from Life*
Ai Xuan (Song dynasty)
Ink and color on silk
Height 23.7 cm × Width 24.3 cm
Palace Museum, Taibei

The poppies drawn from life in this masterpiece of sophisticated brushwork demonstrate their beauty in bloom, thus completely fulfilling the intentions of the artist.

Lotus (*Nelumbo nucifera*)

Does best in pools and ponds or in colored pottery jars from the Guan Kiln and may be enjoyed and appreciated in a courtyard (fig. 62). There should be no vermilion balustrade above the jar. There are rare kinds that may be chosen such as *bingdi* (two lotus flowers on a single stalk), *chongtai*①, *pinzi*②, *simian*③, *bilian* (azure lotus) and *jinbian* (golden border), all good. White lotuses have excellent roots and red ones have fine receptacles. Lotuses should not be planted in seven *dan* (about 700 liter) wine vats or large flower jars.

① *Chongtai*: a variety of lotus where the receptacle is not segmented but the pistil is.

② *Pinzi*: a variety where the flower petals are segmented into three rather like the character *pin* (品).

③ *Simian*: a variety where the flower consists of four segments.

Narcissus

There are two kinds of narcissus (*Narcissus tazetta var. chinensis*). The single-petaled kind with tall flowers but short leaves is the best. They may be planted in numbers in the winter but they are not hardy by nature so the best should be moved to pots and placed on low tables. The remainder may be scattered beneath pines and bamboo or amidst ancient plum blossom and strange stones to achieve the most elegant appearance. Feng Yi took

Fig. 62 *Pure Lotus in Depths of Bamboo*
Qiu Ying
Blue-and-green on paper
Height 18.7 cm × Width 58.1 cm (folding fan format)
Palace Museum, Taibei

In front of a water pavilion, red lotus blossom and leaves are scattered across the surface of a pool. Two scholars sit within the pavilion with a number of antique curios on a table behind them. As they contemplate the lotus blossom they do not forget to handle and appreciate the curios.

eight Daoist concoctions thereby becoming a water sprite (*shuixian*), an elegant name, but the people of the Six dynasties (222–589) used to call it "elegant garlic," a matter for laughter.

Rose Balsam (*Impatiens balsamina*)

Originally called Golden Phoenix Flower, its name was changed to "Good Son and Daughter Flower" by an edict of the Southern Song dynasty (1144–1200) empress Li Fengniang, consort of the Emperor Guangzong (1147–1120), in order to avoid the taboo on phoenix (*feng*) one of her names. The seeds are easily planted but there is nothing particularly attractive about the leaves or flowers. There are those who place five different colored seeds together in a bamboo tube and the flowers blossom in five colors. They believe this to be wonderful. In fact it is nothing to speak of. The red flowers may be used to dye the fingernails but this is not appropriate for a beauty.

Autumn Colors

In the land of Wu the flowers like coxcomb (*Celosia argentea var. cristata*) and *Amaranthus tricolor* are called "autumn colors." In the depths of autumn they blaze with color. They should only be planted in courtyards, since planted in numbers beneath a window they appear too confusing. There is a smaller variety of coxcomb, which is quite rare.

Banana (*Musa basjoo*)

Its green reflects the sunlight at a window, but the shortest are best. If they are tall, the leaves are shredded by the wind (fig. 63). In the winter some people take the stalks, cover then with rice straw and in three years they flower and produce nectar, which is unnecessary. Some put them in pots as *penjing*, which is even more laughable. They are not as elegant as palm trees but make suitable fly whisks or Buddhist prayer mats.

Flowers in Vases

A hall must have flowers in tall vases before it will quicken the interest. But there must be no untidy bunches, no vases of emaciated flowers, no incense or smoke or lamp fuel to blacken them, no grasping with greasy hands, no vases filled with well water since its flavor is not suited to flowers, no drinking of the flower water in the vases, for the water from plum blossom and

Fig. 63 Bananas are often planted and curious stones erected outside a window in the gardens of Jiangnan, thus according with the concept of "banana leaves reflecting green upon small windows" found in Ji Cheng's (1582–?) *Craft of Gardens*.

begonia is very poisonous. If sulfur is placed in the vases during the winter, the water will not freeze (fig. 64).

Penjing (Bonsai)

Nowadays, the fashion is to display *penjing* on low tables. Displaying them in courtyards and pavilions takes second place. I take the opposite view. The best and most elegantly antique is the *Pinus taiwanensis*, no higher than two *chi* (about 60 cm) and no lower than one *chi* (about 30 cm). Its trunk resembles

Fig. 64 *Painting of Autumn Flowers in a Gallbladder-Shaped Pot* (detail)
Anon. (Song dynasty)
Ink and color on silk
Height 26.5 cm × Width 27.5 cm
Palace Museum, Beijing

Flower arrangement in China pays particular attention to beauty of line and natural positioning. No matter whether the material for the arrangement may have been personalized and no matter the shape and material of the container, all conform to natural beauty, the fundamental of Chinese flower arrangement whilst also being filled with a poetic charm.

an arm and the needles are profuse. It has the qualities of "crooked and bent" in the paintings of the Southern Song dynasty painter Ma Yuan, "a fist emerging from the mist" in the paintings of the Northern Song dynasty painter Guo Xi (c. 1000–c. 1090), "spreading layers" in the paintings of the Southern Song dynasty painter Liu Songnian (c. 1131–1218), and "creeping and soaring" in those of Sheng Zizhao (dates unknown) of the Yuan dynasty. Grown in a fine vessel its elegant disorder is very attractive. There is also the elegant and ancient long-lasting plum blossom tree, with bark split like fish scales, covered in green moss, hanging with lichen, which grows flowers and sprouts leaves. It is long-lasting and also elegant. There is nothing good to be said about the present craze for planting agarwood chips in pots. What interest can there be in producing flowers from a chip? Truly, this is to believe old wives' tales. There are also Chinese wolfberry (*Lycium chinensis*), waxy leaf privet (*Ligustrum quihoui*), wild elm and *Sabina chinensis*, which, if the roots resemble dragons or serpents and bear no sign of binding or saw tooth marks, are all treasures.

Next are the water bamboo[①] from Fujian Province and *Damnacanthus indicus* from Hangzhou, which lie somewhere between elegant and vulgar. There is the *Acorus gramineus*, beloved of the immortals, which planted amongst stones is slender but planted in earth is coarse. It is extremely difficult to grow. The people of the land of Wu wash the roots in water and trim them and believe that the early morning dew on the leaves may be used to bathe the eyes. They value it highly. I think that it may be planted in a small courtyard paved with stone and when it glistens after rain it will give off

① Water bamboo: botanical name awaiting confirmation.

Fig. 65 *Paintings in Imitation of Antiquity* (one leaf)
Chen Hongshou (1598–1652)
Ink on paper
Height 17.8 cm × Width 17.8 cm
Metropolitan Museum of Art, New York

This (*penjing*) or miniature potted garden, depicted in just a few brushstrokes, expresses to its utmost the concept of "though made by man the garden seems opened by heaven."

a natural fragrance; in particular it should not be grown as *penjing*, as with the flat peach and double peach, one dare not follow vulgar taste.

Others, such as the orchids and cymbidium of spring, magnolia coco, orange daylily and *Nerium indicum* of summer, the yellow and honey colored chrysanthemum of autumn, the short leaved narcissus and *Canna indica* of winter, may be enjoyed at any time.

The best pots are patinated bronze, the white ware from the Ding Kiln, and ware from the Guan and Ge kilns. New products such as colored wares from the Guan Kiln and the ware manufactured by Gong Chun may be used but the rest is of no account. Pots should be round not square, in particular they should not be long and narrow. Lingbi stone, Ying stone and Xishan stone may be used as an accompaniment but the rest are also of no account. One or two pots may be arranged in a studio but no more. Small pots should not be placed on vermilion stands nor large ones on bricks from the Guan Kiln. For the best, one should seek out old stone benches or ancient lotus plinths as stands (fig. 65).

CHAPTER THREE
WATER AND ROCKS

Stone endows man with antiquity and water endows him with a peaceful remoteness. Above all, without water and stone a garden cannot exist. Water must wind and twist and stones stand high, and all must be suitably laid out. One outcrop may become like Huashan Mountain (in Huayin City of Shaanxi Province) in height and breadth and a single ladleful of water may turn into a multitude of rivers and lakes. Bamboo must be planted with ancient trees, strange creeping vines and misshapen trees crisscrossed and towering over all, with heights of deepest blue and jade-green streams and rushing spring torrents as if in the uttermost depths of a ravine, all enough to create a place of distinction. This is but a mere indication, not all needs to be like this in detail.

Broad Pools

Pools may be excavated by the *mu* or *qing*, the broader the better. Terraces and waterside pavilions may be erected in the midst of the largest, or dikes and dams with reeds (*Phragmites communis*) and sweetflag (*Acorus*

Fig. 66 *Early Spring* (detail)
Guo Xi
Ink and color on silk
Height 158.3 cm × Width 108.1 cm
Palace Museum, Taibei

This painting portrays the imminent arrival of spring. Mountain peaks soar in distant majesty and strange and curious rock formations stand bone-like in the foreground. The space between is occupied by woods and trees, dense here and scattered there, each different in shape and posture. A spring stream tumbles down the mountain to join the river below where pavilions and buildings lie half-hidden. Chinese garden landscapes are built to imitate this kind of natural scenery and to encapsulate it in the space of a small garden.

calamus) growing in their midst, a view without limit, truly a great expanse of water (fig. 67). To achieve an ordered beauty, the banks should be built from patterned stone set about with vermilion railings. No mounds of earth should be left like the vulgar so-called "fishing battle stations" from which nets are cast or those imitations of Jinshan Mountain and Jiaoshan Mountain rising from the river opposite each other. Weeping willows should be planted by the water but with no peach or apricot trees amongst them. Ducks and geese may be raised, about ten to a flock to be of any interest. At the widest point a water pavilion may be built, for the best looking like those in paintings; there should be no huts on rafts. Lotus flowers may be grown beside the bank with split bamboo as a fence to prevent the lotus plants spreading. They should not cover the whole pond and obscure sight of the water.

Fig. 67 *The Studio of True Appreciation* (detail)

Small Pools

A small pool may be dug out in the front of steps but it must be surrounded by Taihu stone and the water must be clear so that the bottom may be seen (fig. 68). Goldfish may be kept, swimming amongst aquatic grass for your amusement and the pool should be set about with slender bamboo and wild wisteria. If the pool can be dug a little deeper, the flow of water from the spring will be even better. Square, round and octagonal shapes are to be avoided.

Waterfalls

Living in the hills where water flows down from above makes it easier to create waterfalls. If one wishes to make one in a garden, different lengths of bamboo should be cut to carry the flow of water from the eaves and then joined and concealed between stones broken with a pickaxe and piled high. A small pool may be dug below to receive the water

Fig. 68 Summer Rock in the Isolated Garden
The Isolated Garden in Yangzhou in Jiangsu Province is one of the Four Great Gardens of China famous for the artistry of its rock building. The way in which the four "false mountains" representing spring, summer, autumn and winter have been built with different kinds of rock combines the art of garden architecture with landscape painting. The Summer Rock is surrounded by piled Taihu stones and the center is occupied by a lotus pond where lotus leaves are gathered together. Behind the rock structure a delicately built pavilion stands in exquisite tranquility.

and in it one may place stones so that when it rains they cause the waterfall to rush roaring on, an amazing sight. Waterfalls may be well-placed amongst pines and bamboos, and in the crisp green shade they look even better. Some people collect water in pools at the top of a hill, and when there are guests, release the water through a sluice so that it pours down from above. However, this can never surpass the flow of rainwater from the eaves in elegance because it is artificial. Only the flow of rainwater is close to nature.

Digging a Well

Water from a well is turbid and is unsuitable for cooking and making tea, but it is indispensable for rinsing inkstones, polishing furniture and watering flowers and bamboo. Wells should be dug beneath bamboos, deep enough to see the spring water and equipped with a windlass to raise it. A small pavilion may be erected over it as well (fig. 69). A large simple stone balustrade in the old style and known to the ancients as a "silver bed" may be erected round it. Wells have spirits, and a small stone altar may be erected at the well side where goblets of clear water may be dedicated to them to create an atmosphere of true elegance.

Natural Water

Rainwater that falls in autumn is the best, with the rains of early summer the next. Autumn rain tastes crisp and pure and the rains of early summer pure and sweet. As between winter and spring rain, spring is the better as spring is balmy and the rain moist. The rain of summer storms is unsuitable since it is caused by the dragons of tempest and thunder, more

than able to bring harm to man. Snow is the essence of the five grains and may be used to make tea, an elegant affair, though fresh snow has an earthy flavor and must be left to stand for a little before it is at its best. Rainwater may be strained through cloth in a receptacle in the courtyard. Water from gutters should not be used.

Underground Springs

Natural springs that flow like the springs of Huishan (at Wuxi in present day Jiangsu Province) are the best. The next best are springs that flow both clear and cold. There is no difficulty in finding a clear spring. The difficulty lies in finding one that is cold as

Fig. 69 *A Gathering for Tea at Mount Hui* (detail)
Wen Zhengming
Ink and color on paper
Height 21.9 cm × Length 67 cm
Palace Museum, Beijing

The painting shows Wen Zhengming and a group of friends boiling spring water and tasting tea as well as reciting poetry while on a tour of Mount Hui in Wuxi in Jiangsu Province. The arrangement of the pavilion roof, well, and trees and stones within the painting seems to precisely match the literary descriptions.

well. Where the spring is muddy, it will be neither clear nor cold. There are also springs that are fragrant and sweet though it is easy to find sweetness and difficult to find fragrance. There are none that are just clear but not sweet. The water that rushes over waterfalls is not to be drunk, for taken often it gives you a headache, like the scenic waters of Lushan Mountain and the waterfalls of Tiantai Mountain (present day Tiantai in Zhejiang Province), which are fit only for ears and eyes and not the tongue. Water from hot springs that contain sulfur is not suitable for drinking.

Flowing Water

River water must be taken from places remote from human habitation. The Nanling spring (outside the Jinshan Temple at Zhenjiang in present day Jiangsu Province) bursts forth from between rocks and is thus regarded as

being of the first order. Where the spring water meets the main flow it must settle until it is clear before it can be drunk.

Cinnabar Springs

Amongst the peaks and rivers where Daoist immortals and elders practice self-improvement, there is cinnabar in the water. It has a strange taste but can lengthen life and cure illness. This natural liquid cinnabar is not easy to find.

Grades of Stone

Of the stone used in gardening, Lingbi stone is the best with Ying stone next. Nevertheless, both kinds are extremely valuable and difficult to buy. The larger kind is particularly difficult to obtain. Those that are more than a few *chi* (one *chi* equals about 30 cm) may be regarded

as treasures. The small ones may be placed on tables. The very best are those that gleam like lacquer and tinkle like jade. Heng stone has a wax colored ground and those shaped like the topmost tip of a mountain are the best. People say, "There are no peaks to Lingbi stone and no slopes on Ying stone." As I see it this is not so. Other stones are coarsely patterned and utterly without curves or twists or towering precipitous peaks. More recently people have been using large pieces of cinnabar stone, azurite, and peacock stone to make inkstones in the shape of mountains and pots. This is vulgar.

Lingbi Stone

Lingbi stone comes from Lingbi county in Anhui Province. It can be found by digging in the gravel deep in the hills. There is a kind, without holes, that is delicately patterned in white, like jade. The best, like those shaped

like reclining oxen or hornless dragons (*chi*) and all manner of other strange forms, may be termed true curios.

Ying Stone

Ying stone comes from Yingde in Guangdong Province where nodules of stone grow on rocky surfaces from whence they are sawn off, hence the ridged serrations on the bottom of the stone. The stones can reach a height of three *chi* (about 90 cm) though small ones are just over a *cun* (about 3 cm). They look very imposing piled into a miniature mountain in front of a studio. However, by reason of distance they are difficult to obtain.

Taihu Stone

Taihu stone found in water is treasured because, over time, it has been buffeted by waves that have pierced it with holes to produce an exquisite appearance (fig. 70). When found in the hills it is known as "dry stone" and has a very rough texture. Where man-made holes have been worn away by time, and the axe marks have disappeared, it presents an elegant appearance. The artificial mountains so popular in the land of Wu are all built with this stone. There are also small stones long-immersed in the lake that have been caught in fishermen's nets and are very similar to Lingbi and Ying stones but they do not possess the same purity of sound.

Fig. 70 *The Studio of True Appreciation* (detail)
Wen Zhengming
Ink and color on paper
Height 36 cm × Length 107.8 cm
Shanghai Museum

This is a painting of a building called the Studio of True Appreciation, half-hidden amongst trees where, on a table inside, all manner of objects for the studio are set out and two scholars sit across from each other. The building is surrounded by Taihu stones, all of different shapes. The painting is brushed in a pale ink that perfectly conveys the limpid natural qualities of the Taihu stones.

Yaofeng Stone

This stone from the Yaofeng Mountain (near Suzhou in present day Jiangsu Province) was only found recently. The stone is covered by a profusion of moss and it has an attractively simple appearance. Since it has not been mined before there is much of it, though it is by no means delicate or exquisite. But it is this very lack of delicacy that makes it so good.

Kunshan Stone

Kunshan stone comes from the Ma'an Moutain (present day Kunshan in Jiangsu Province) and can be obtained by excavation. The white one is the best. There are two kinds: "chicken bone" and "walnut" but they are vulgar in taste and not objects of any elegance. Sometimes they measure up to seven or eight *chi* in height (over two meters) and may be placed in large stone jars. The Ma'an Mountain contains much flint and the temperature is warm, so that the sweetflag that grows there flourishes. However, these stones cannot be placed on tables or in pots and dishes.

Jinchuan, Jiangle and Yangdu Stones

These three kinds of stone, Jinchuan stone (from Linghai County in Liaoning Province),

Fig. 71 *In Imitation of the Brushwork of Mi Fu's White Clouds over the Xiaoxiang River*
Dong Qichang (1555–1636)
Ink on paper
Height 29.3 cm × Length 340.8 cm
Liaoning Provincial Museum

Mi Fu was one of the great calligraphers of the Northern Song dynasty. He creatively developed the techniques of his predecessors and in his paintings of *shanshui* (landscape-type scenes) employed an ink dot process that fully realized the smudging effect of ink to produce an air of poetic grace. His particular qualities were fully absorbed by his successors. This painting by Dong Qichang is a brushed ink painting of the scenery of Lake Dongting that borrows the essence of Mi Fu's landscape style to display a scene of vague and indistinct mistiness.

Jiangle stone (from Nanping in Fujian Province) and Yangdu (sheep's gut) stone are the lowest grade of all, Jinchuan stone being the most detestable. Whenever I see an artificial mountain with some of these stones scattered on top I wonder, "Where is the taste in that?" Elegance in this kind of stone lies in the large simple looking stone quarried by axe. A single stone set up on its own is exceptionally ugly.

Chalcedony

Chalcedony is produced at Yizhou (present day Linyi in Shandong Province). It is patterned like agate. The best is rich in red and is fine and glossy. There is also stone with red patterning on a white ground and bamboo leaf agate

with a striped pattern resembling a bamboo leaf, hence the name. These may all be sawn into slivers and inlaid into tables, couches and screens. They are not valuable. Stones of five colors, as large as a fist or as small as a bean in the shape of fish and birds and beasts and the human form or an overlapping square, as well as key patterning (derived from the character 回), are pleasing when placed in a small blue and green pot or a white pot from the Xuande Kiln①. They are extremely valuable and difficult to obtain and thus not many should be displayed in a studio. I have recently seen people who set out several pots of them just like a street stall. In the capital (Beijing) there is a "Studio of the Drunken Stone" where I hear that there is a very fine collection of strange stones. In the mountain streams of Yizhou there are also stones of pure red and pure green, which make good curios.

> ① The Xuande Kiln: erected in the Xuande era (1426–1435) of Ming dynasty. Its porcelain is fine and delicate with fresh glowing colors. Small pieces are particularly fine. The colors come in bright red, ruby red, sweet white, and kingfisher blue. The most valuable is a bright red.

Dali Marble

Dali marble comes from the town of Dali in Yunnan, the best has the whiteness of jade or the blackness of ink. White tinged with greenish blue and black tinged with grey are lesser grades. Nevertheless, nothing can exceed the quality, if one can obtain it, of old stone, the surface of which presents the natural form of a misty landscape such as those by the Northern Song painter Mi Fu (1051–1107). The ancients used this stone to inlay screens. It is only recently that it has been used for tables and couches, this by no means ancient. In Jingkou (present day Zhenjiang in Jiangsu Province) there has recently been a kind of stone that resembles Dali marble but the patterning is not distinct. However, when mineral powder is added to the cracks to form a landscape pattern it fetches a high price. It is not difficult to distinguish true from false and the old are the most valuable of the genuine pieces.

Yong Stone

Yong stone, that is to say Qiyang stone, comes from the territory of Chu (Lingling in present day Hunan Province). It is not very dense and stones of good coloring bear representations of hills, water, sun, moon and people. Stones with purple patterning are a little better than others but most of them have been carved with a blade and are not natural. Once in the hand, the unevenness of the surface is apparent. Large ones are good for making screens.

CHAPTER FOUR
BIRDS AND FISH

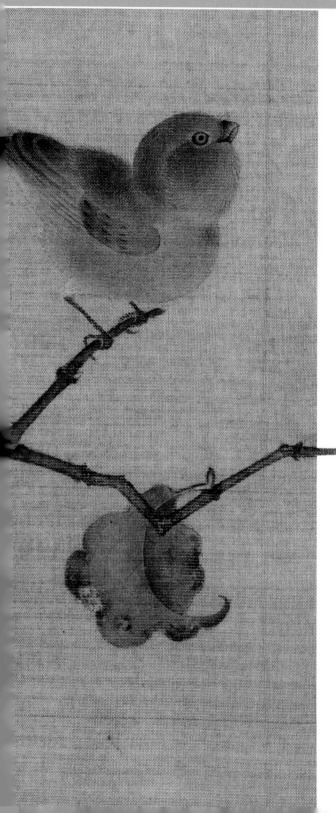

Songbirds brush the eaves in flight and fish dart through the waterweed, men of elegance and taste, apprehending their nature, do not weary of watching them all day long. Hence they observe the sight and sound and feeding habits of birds and fish; in the distance, one nests while the other sleeps in the sand or swims by the bank, disporting itself abroad and floating in the depths. Nearer still, bramblings, magpies, roosters, orioles and crows are countless in their kinds. How can the common herd be permitted to trespass amongst the red-leafed woods and clear waters? Thus, one must choose the noble and refined and provide a number of kinds to enjoy and instruct a boy to raise them, familiarizing himself with their nature, or one may train birds and befriend the wild ducks and fish, a necessary art for those who live in solitude amongst the hills and woods.

Fig. 72 *When the Fruit Is Ripe the Birds Arrive* (detail)
Lin Chun (Southern Song dynasty)
Ink and color on silk
Height 26.9 cm × Width 27.2 cm
Palace Museum, Beijing

The fruit is already fully ripe on the branch and a small bird perches on a twig as if about to spread its wings in flight. The artist vividly depicts the yellow-green leaves, the pale red fruit and the light yellow bird. The painting is not large but it holds a perception of the appeal of nature. The sight of a scene such as this would gladden the heart of one living in the hills as a hermit.

Crane

The cranes from Crane's Nest Village in Huating (Songjiang in present day Shanghai) are majestic in their bearing. They have feet of green patterned like the cracks of a turtle's shell and are to be admired the most. There are also cranes at Hejin of Jiangling (present day Hubei Province), and Weiyang (present day Yangzhou in Jiangsu Province). In choosing cranes one should select those of majestic appearance and dignified bearing with a clear call, slender neck and strong but fine feet. When they stand like people the back

Fig. 73 *The Garden of the Humble Administrator, Album Leaf*

Wen Zhengming
Ink on paper
Height 26.4 cm × Width 27.3 cm
Metropolitan Museum of Art, New York

The artist attended the construction of the Humble Administrator's Garden in Suzhou and compiled a descriptive album of 31 paintings with accompanying poems. He later prepared another album of 12 of these paintings of which this painting is one (now only eight leaves remain in the museum). The leaf below shows a grove of bamboos growing outside a room in which two scholars sit gazing at the scene outside. A bird, possibly a crane, stands in front of one of the clusters of bamboo. Hermits in the company of a crane, reciting poetry, and painting is an elegant sight indeed.

should be straight. They should be raised on a spacious terrace or earthen mound where a straw hut has been built to house them, close to a pool and marshy ground. They should be fed on fish and grain. To teach them to dance, hold back their food and put it out in the open wild and let a boy stamp his feet and clap his hands to attract them. In the course of time the cranes will dance as soon as they hear the sound of clapping, this is called "training through food." For those who live in the remote wild, amongst the rocks and pines, only the sacred crane will suit, other feathered families do not count (fig. 73).

Xichi Ducks

This duck, slightly larger than the mandarin duck (*Aix galericulata*), has a magic command of the water and thus cannot be harmed by its other inhabitants. It should be raised in broad expanses of water where it forms flocks. It has a red beak and green plumage and floats on the water in all its brilliance. Others, like the black-billed white-feathered duck, may be raised in ones and twos instead of geese.

Fig. 74 *A Many-Colored Parrot* (detail)
Zhao Ji (Song Emperor Huizong, 1082–1135)
Ink and color on silk
Height 53.3 cm × Width 125.1 cm
Museum of Fine Arts, Boston

The painting shows two sprays of apricot blossoms. A many-colored parrot perches in profile on a twig of one of the sprays. Its beak, eyes, wings, and claws are delineated in meticulous detail and the natural vitality of the whole is extremely attractive.

A flock of water birds swimming beneath the weeping willows and curving balustrades is a joy to behold.

Parrot

Parrots can talk and need to be taught poems and rhymes, they should not be instructed in the coarse speech of markets and alleys that can so unpleasantly fill the ear. Their feeding perches and food bowl should be neatly made (fig. 74). However, this bird together with golden pheasants, peacocks, the collared finchbill (*Spizixos semitorques*) and the Chinese tragopan (*Tragopan caboti*) are all objects for the women's quarters and not something for the secluded gentleman of discriminating taste.

Fig. 75 *Myna Bird on an Autumn Tree* (detail)
Anon. (Song dynasty)
Ink and color on silk
Height 25 cm × Width 26.5 cm
Palace Museum, Beijing

A myna bird perches on a tree, its sharp claws gripping the branch firmly, its head turned and eyes askance as if listening carefully. The myna's expression is keen and its posture imposing. The tail feathers are neat and the plumage is a gleaming black. The texture and gradation of different parts of the plumage is fully expressed through the brushwork.

cinnabar of Chenzhou (the northern part of Huaihua in present day Hunan Province) (fig. 76). This kind is the most suitable to be displayed in bowls. The red ones with a touch of yellow may only be displayed in pools and ponds.

Kinds of Fish

To begin with, people esteemed pure red and pure white. Thereafter it was Gold and Grey (a white body with the character 王 in red on the head), Golden Saddle (white head and tail with a band of gold round the belly), Brocade (red and white intertwined like a brocade sash, no dorsal fin, body of many colors), Seal-Head Red (white body, a mark on the head in red like a square seal), Towel-Head Red (white body, head colored red), Red Cheek (white body, head and both cheeks red), Head and Tail Red

Chinese Blackbird, Laughing Thrush, Crested Myna

The Chinese blackbird (*Turdus merula mandarinus*), laughing thrush (Chinese *huamei—Garrulax canorus*) and crested myna (*Acridotheres cristatellus*) (fig. 75) will, after training, speak and sing gently in many ways that are pleasant to the ear but they are not suitable for the secluded studio. However, they may be displayed for show in finely carved cages and on decorated balustrades in the corridor. These birds are most appreciated in the land of Wu. I believe that those whose hobby is the raising of birds should seek out tall trees in deep forest in which to hear the natural singing of birds, for that is to be treasured the most. There is another small bird called the siskin (*Carduelis spinus*), which is aggressive by nature, of inelegant appearance and is particularly not to be spoken of.

Goldfish

The rearing of goldfish flourishes in the land of Wu alone and they take the name from the

Fig. 76 Stem Bowl with a Pattern of Three Fish in Underglaze Red

Ming dynasty, Xuande period
Height 8.8 cm, diameter at mouth 9.9 cm, diameter at foot 4.4 cm
Palace Museum, Beijing

This dignified stem bowl is glazed in white overall with a raised decoration of three red fish on its outer surface. The lively portrayal of the fish makes them appear as if following each other through the water head to tail.

(head and tail both red), and Crane's Top Red (white body, a red mark on the head, no dorsal fin). Following on, people esteemed Ink Eye (the eyes protruding beyond the socket and the eye colored dark black with red patterning), Snow Eye (red body, protruding eyes of a whitish red color), Vermilion Eye (white body, protruding purple eyes with a reddish vermilion cast), Purple Eye (white body, protruding eyes colored purple with red patterning), Agate Eye and Amber Eye (both white body, amber colored protruding eyes), Gold Sheath (gold colored tail) and Silver Sheath (white colored tail); all were reckoned at the time to be exceptionally valuable. There were also Jade Speckled Gold (completely pure white body with red dots on the back), Falling Flowers and Flowing Water (whole body covered in flower petal stripes), Eight-Petaled Lotus (white or red body with a chrysanthemum-shaped lump on the head), Cutting Away the Red Dust (body half red, half white or one side red, one side white), Jade Band (red head and tail, a band of white round the waist), Plum Blossom Strip (white body, red head with a red plum blossom-shaped lump on the head or the other way round), Wave Pattern (completely white body with inlaid red patterning in the form of waves or the other way round), and Seven Star Pattern (body completely white with a pattern in red on the back representing the seven stars of the Big Dipper or the other way round. It is difficult to describe them all and since they have been named at will, there is no fixed form.

Blue Goldfish and White Goldfish

Kingfisher blue and snow white; on close inspection their innards are visible. This is a variety of the goldfish that is extremely valuable.

Fishtails

These range from two to nine in number and all may be found. But to invest all the beauty in the tail endangers the body as a whole. The body must be firm and delicate with bone and flesh in balance and the colors fresh before it can be reckoned up to standard.

Viewing Fish

This is best done early, before sunrise, when, whether in bowl or pool, fish dart through the crystal clear water. One can also view fish under the cool light of the moon when the fish turn and leap in its reflected light, rousing eye and ear. There are other favorable situations in which to view fish, as for example when a gentle breeze lightly brushes the water in a poetry of its own, or as the water rises after rain like the pattern of ripples in silk.

Clearing Mud

Mud accumulates at the bottom of the bowl one or two days after the water has been changed. It may be cleared using a tube of speckled bamboo. If it is not cleared for some time, colors turn dull which is why valuable fish may not be raised in ponds.

Water Jars

There is an ancient kind of water jar made of copper that can hold two *dan* (about 200 liters) and is clad in copper on its four sides. It is not known for what purpose it was used in antiquity, it may be that oil was poured into the holes and it was used as a lamp. Today, however, it is used for raising fish and is most elegantly antique. Next is the colored ware marked Palace Manufactory and the pure white ware of the Cizhou (Ci County in present day Hebei Province) and Guan Kiln, which may be used. The only kind that may not be used is the decorated ware of Yixing (in present day Jiangsu Province) and the vulgar looking seven-*dan* (about 700 liters) ox foot jars. My reason for presenting all these is to provide examples for appreciation; sticking rigidly to the rules results in vulgarity.

CHAPTER FIVE
CALLIGRAPHY AND PAINTING

Gold is mined in the hills and pearls are produced from the depths, they are inexhaustible and valued by all beneath heaven. Thus, calligraphy and painting, having existed in the universe for so long and yet artists of note only able to live a single life, how much more should they be similarly collected and treasured? Once in the hands of the vulgar they are mishandled, their pages disordered and torn, a disaster for true calligraphy and painting. Consequently there is collection without discrimination, discrimination without the capacity to enjoy, enjoyment without the ability to remount and repair, and repair without the ability to order and select. None of this can be true collection. Moreover, in the collection of so much, good and bad become intermingled, thus the order of quality must be established and free of confusion. To display the genuine with the false and the new with the old is tantamount to buying from the stall of a barbarian bookseller and where lies the interest in that? A collection should contain good examples of the Jin, Tang, Song and Yuan dynasties before it can be considered to demonstrate a grasp of antiquity. It is truly a bad habit to pursue the collection of recent paper and ink, to compare the value of genuine and false without any real appreciation, to rely on what is said rather than what is seen and always to mention price when handling a scroll.

Fig. 77 *Travelers amongst Mountains and Streams*
Fan Kuan (950–1032)
Ink on silk
Height 206.3 cm × Width 103.3 cm
Palace Museum, Taibei

The greater part of this painting is occupied by lofty, towering mountains. The mountain peaks are covered with luxuriant vegetation and trees and in the valley depths waterfalls send the water cascading downwards. Steep rocks fall away from the summit and in the foreground a river races by. A column of men and horses follows the course of the river along a mountain path adding a sign of life to the empty stillness. The composition of this painting is unique and the straightforward honesty of the artist's powerful brushwork projects a majestic grandeur, so that the Ming artist Dong Qichang described it as "the very first of all Song paintings."

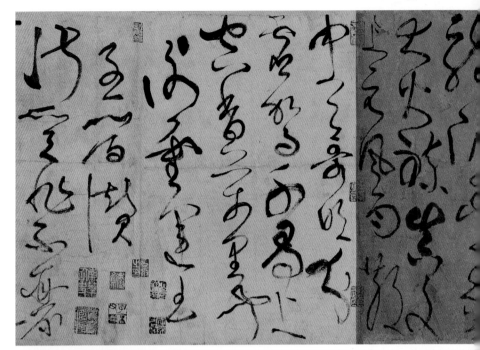

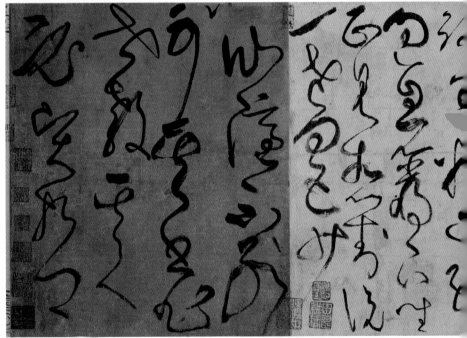

Fig. 78 *Four Classical Verses* (detail)
Zhang Xu (c. 675–c. 750)
Wild cursive script (188 characters in 40 lines)
Paper base
Height 29.5 × Length 195.2 cm
Liaoning Provincial Museum

In China, calligraphy is a unique art form that expresses the beauty of the Chinese script. From the oracle bone inscriptions on tortoiseshells, through the development of seal script (*zhuanshu*) and clerical script (*lishu*) to the later cursive (*caoshu*), regular (*kaishu*) and semi-cursive (*xingshu*) scripts, all displayed their own particular artistic fascination. During the Tang dynasty, Zhang Xu made his name as a practitioner of cursive script and this is the only surviving example of his work. The brush strokes are powerful, opulent and full of vigor. The style is as unrestrained as the wind and waves at sea and yet as delicate as mist. It is the very summit of cursive script.

On Calligraphy

One must contemplate the calligraphy of the ancients with a clear mind and settled heart. First, observe the construction of the brushstrokes and how they reflect and relate to the spirit of the calligrapher, then observe whether it be natural or forced; next examine the inscriptions old and new at the end of the piece or painting together with its provenance, then the seals of the collectors and finally the color of the paper or silk. Where there is construction but no "tip" to the calligraphy it is an imitation; where there is spirit to the brushwork but no sense of place it is a copy; where the brushstrokes

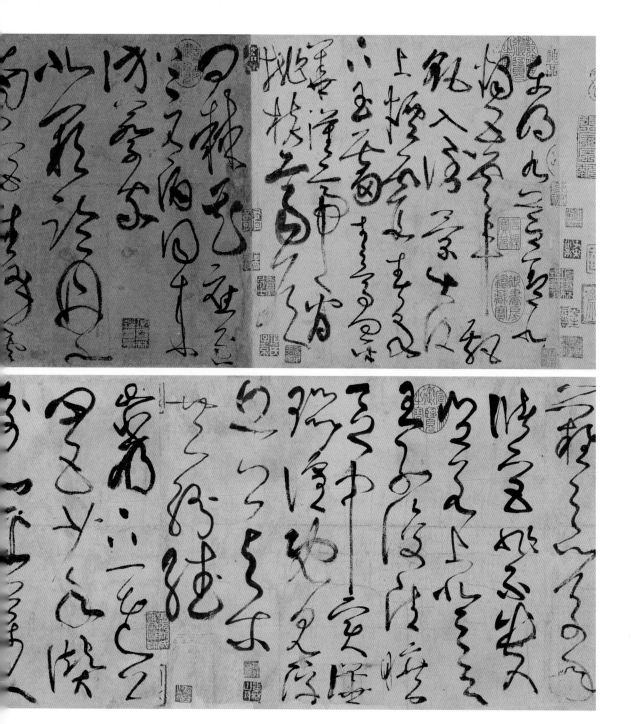

seem unconnected
and the shape of
the characters
seems as dead as
an abacus bead it
is a copy from a
rubbing; where
the outline① of the

① Outlining: When the
calligraphers of the Tang
dynasty engraved their
calligraphy on stone, they
marked both edges of the
brushstrokes with fine
lines thus outlining thick
and thin strokes with no
loss of reality.

characters exists but the spirit and color is
lackluster it is mere outlining. In their use
of ink, whether moist, dry, thick or thin,
the ancients always penetrated to the fibers
of the paper or silk; with later forgeries the
brushwork appears to float on the surface
and they are not difficult to distinguish
(fig. 78).

On Painting

Landscapes take first place (fig. 79), then
bamboo, trees, orchids and stone, followed
by figures (fig. 80), birds and beasts, buildings
and palaces and small houses, with large
houses last of all. Figures should be active,
flowers and fruit should sway in the wind,
birds, beasts, insects and fish should be lifelike,
hills, woods and streams should be broad and
leisurely, dwellings should be hidden away,
bridges must cross back and forth, rocks and
stone be ancient and moist, water clear and
bright, and mountains imposing. Streams
should splash and flow, cloud and mist should
appear and vanish, paths in the wild twist and
turn, pine branches grow crooked, bamboos
be enveloped in mist and rain, the feet of
mountains descend into clear water and the
sources of spring water be apparent. With all
these characteristics, even though the artist
may be unknown, the work is indeed by
the hand of a master. If, on the contrary, the
figures are lifeless, flowers and fruit resemble
carvings, insects, fish, birds and beasts mere
shapes, landscapes, woods and springs are
clogged in composition, buildings and palaces
a confused mess, bridges broken, paths neither

Top
Fig. 79   *A Thousand Li of Mountains and Rivers*
(detail)
Wang Ximeng (Northern Song dynasty)
Ink and color on silk
Height 51.5 cm × Length 1191.5 cm
Palace Museum, Beijing

The landscape painting, the depiction of the scenery
of the natural landscape, is a substantial component
of Chinese painting. It gradually evolved into a
major branch of painting from the Sui (581–618)
and Tang dynasties onwards and concentrates upon
the expression of the conceptual management of the
placement of objects on the surface of a painting. In
this painting ranges of mountains rise and fall and
swathes of mist cover the rivers in an atmosphere of
magnificent vastness. In this single scroll, gorgeous
colors and meticulous brushwork display the majesty
of hills and rivers in a work that has long been
regarded as one of the masterpieces
of Song dynasty blue-green
landscape painting.

level nor steep, roads without a
trace of entry or exit, rocks flat and
lifeless, trees lacking branches and
leaves and where there is no balance
between height and size nor distinction
between near and far, or there is unsuitable
shading, or incompetent additions, or no
water surface at the foot of a mountain and no
discernible source for spring water, then even

though there may be a famous signature, it is bound to be from a vulgar brush and added later. As to copies by a different hand, the fall of the ink and the application of color will lack the elegance of the antique and are not difficult to detect.

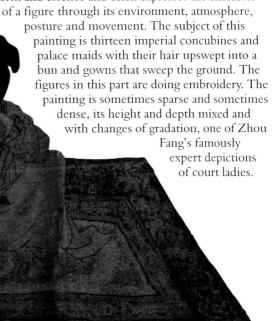

Fig. 80 *Court Ladies with Fans* (detail)
Attributed to Zhou Fang (Tang dynasty)
Ink and color on silk
Height 33.7 cm × Width 204.8 cm
Palace Museum, Beijing

"Figure painting" emerged as a class of painting in China earlier than landscapes or flowers-and-birds. It differs from Western portraiture in that it seeks both form and essence and often expresses the character of a figure through its environment, atmosphere, posture and movement. The subject of this painting is thirteen imperial concubines and palace maids with their hair upswept into a bun and gowns that sweep the ground. The figures in this part are doing embroidery. The painting is sometimes sparse and sometimes dense, its height and depth mixed and with changes of gradation, one of Zhou Fang's famously expert depictions of court ladies.

The Value of Calligraphy and Painting

In the value of calligraphy, regular script is the standard. For example, one hundred characters of cursive script by Wang Xizhi are equal to one line of semi-cursive script and three lines of semi-cursive script are equal to one line of regular script. However, pieces such as his *Expeditions of General Yue Yi, The Yellow Court Classic, In Praise of Painting* and *Statement of Pledge* should be taken as a whole and cannot be priced by the character. Paintings are valued the same way: landscapes, bamboo and rocks together with depictions of ancient worthies may be treated as if regular script, whilst smaller examples of figures and flowers-and-birds equal semi-cursive script (fig. 81). Large figures and depictions of gods and Buddhas, palaces and pavilions, beasts, insects and fish, are the equivalent of cursive script. Nevertheless, terrace pavilion wall paintings of loyal and upright ministers and paintings of past sages and virtuous women on palace walls that speak to the soul and are in touch with the gods, or resemble the painting of Gu Kaizhi that miraculously disappeared from within a locked box, or Zhang Sengyou of the Southern dynasties painting of dragons that was so lifelike it seemed to fly from the very wall—all with a touch of the miraculous —are treasures beyond price. Painting is a refined pursuit. Once it becomes illusory, freakish and rootless, no matter whether ancient or modern, it must lose a place.

Ancient and Modern Good and Bad

It is the period that determines the quality of calligraphy. The Six dynasties are not as good as the Jin dynasty and the Wei (220–265),

Fig. 81 *Lotus in Water*
Anon. (Song dynasty)
Ink and color on silk
Height 23.8 cm × Width 25 cm
Palace Museum, Beijing

Flowers-and-birds is a class of Chinese painting that depicts flowers, birds, and insects. This painting is a fine example of the genre. The whole painting is occupied by a single pink lotus blossom. The application of color possesses a stylish dignity. At the same time, the shape, angle, coloring and sense of light of each petal has been carefully arranged to perfectly produce that gentlemanly concept of the lotus as "emerging unsullied from mud."

Song and Yuan dynasties are not the equal of the Six dynasties and the Tang dynasty. All paintings are not the same: in Buddhism and Daoism, figures, court ladies, horses and oxen, the modern does not approach the ancient but in landscapes, woods and rocks, flowers and bamboo, birds and fish, the ancient does not approach the modern. For example, the works of Gu Kaizhi, Lu Tanwei and Zhang Sengyou, Wu Daozi (c. 680–759), Yan Lide (c. 596–656) and Yan Liben (c. 601–673) of the Tang dynasty are simple, straightforward and natural in character, while the works of Zhou Fang, Han Gan (dates unknown) (fig. 82) and Dai Song (dates unknown) also of the Tang dynasty are beyond imagination in their style and strength and have never been surpassed by later scholars.

In the Five dynasties (907–960), Guan Tong (907–960) of the Later Liang period (554–587) and Xu Xi (dates unknown) of the Southern Tang period (937–975), Huang Quan (?–965), Huang Jucai (933–?) and Li Cheng (919–967), Fan Kuan, Dong Yuan (?–c. 962), father and son Mi Fu and Mi Youren (1074–1153) of the Northern Song dynasty, Zhao Mengfu (1254–1322), Huang Gongwang (1269–1354), Ni Zan (c. 1301–1374), Wang Meng of the Yuan dynasty, and the present Ming dynasty's Tang Yin, Shen Zhou, my own grandfather Wen Zhengming and Wen Jia (1501–1583), did not follow a teacher. Their artistry reached a pinnacle nevertheless. Even were the Tang dynasty's

Li Sixun (651–716) and Li Zhaodao (dates unknown), father and son, and Bian Luan (dates unknown) to be reborn they could not compare with them.

Consequently, collectors of calligraphy should seek out the ancient and the collection of paintings should start from Gu Kaizhi, Lu Tanwei, Zhang Sengyou, and Wu Daozi and carry on through to the well-known artists of the Jiajing (1522–1566) and Longqing (1567–1572) periods where there are some impressive examples. As to the calligraphers and artists of the present, I would not be so rash as to venture a criticism.

Sketches

The draft paintings of the ancients were known as sketches (*fenben*) and were lovingly collected by our forbears because of their natural spontaneity. There are many fine examples from the Xuanhe (1119–1125) and Shaoxing (1131–1162) periods.

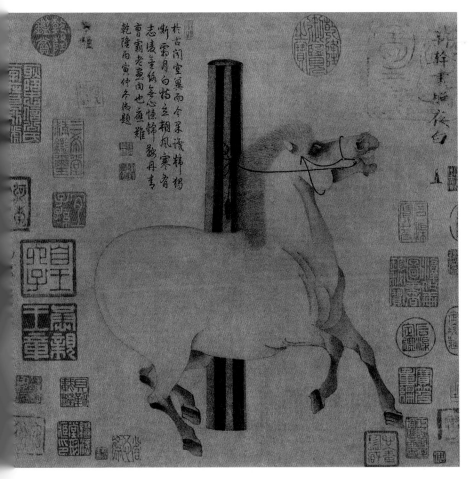

Fig. 82 *Night-Shining White*

Han Gan
Ink on paper
Height 30.8 cm × Width 33.5 cm
Metropolitan Museum of Art, New York

Han Gan was known for his paintings of horses. This painting is of an imperial steed known as Night-Shining White. It is tethered to a post by its nose and is seemingly about to neigh. Its proud unyielding character is visible at a glance.

Connoisseurship

One should look at calligraphy and paintings as one approaches beautiful women: there should be no trace of coarseness to it. The paper and silk of ancient paintings is fragile, scrolls carelessly rolled and unrolled are easily torn, even less should they be exposed to wind and sunlight. Paintings should not be viewed by lamplight lest ash or, worse still, candle grease fall and spoil them; when viewing paintings after wining and dining the hands should be rinsed in clean water; when displaying scrolls they should not be damaged by the fingernails. Matters such as these are too numerous to mention. But when one always desires everything to proceed smoothly without accident and fears to be regarded as putting on airs, then one should only discuss calligraphy and painting with true connoisseurs and those rich in the knowledge of antiquity. With the vulgar and untutored one should keep one's secrets.

Silk

The color of the silk and the smell of the ink in old paintings have a pleasing flavor and fragrance of their own. Images of Buddhas darkened by incense smoke differ in color as between top and bottom. Forgeries, though, are yellow and lackluster in color. Rents in old silk will always resemble the mouth of a carp with two or three threads of trailing silk, but forgeries split neatly. Tang silk is coarse and thick, though there is some that is treated by being pounded smooth. There is also light single-weave silk more than four *chi* (roughly 120 cm) in width. The silk of the Five dynasties is as coarse as ordinary cloth. The academy silk of the Song dynasty is even, thick, and close. There is also a single-weave silk with a breadth of more than five *chi* (roughly 150 cm) as close and fine as paper. Yuan dynasty silk and the Palace Manufactory silk of the present Ming dynasty is the same

as the silk of the Song dynasty. During the Yuan dynasty there was a silk made by the Mi family of Jiaxing (of Zhejiang Province), famed for silk production, which was used by Zhao Mengfu and Sheng Zizhao. This family still produces fine silk today. Recently, Dong Qichang mostly used a white silk rubbed smooth by a stone, which gives it rather an air of superiority.

Imperial Palace Calligraphy and Painting

During the reign of the Song Emperor Huizong, all calligraphy and painting in the imperial collection was inscribed by the emperor in his own hand or later sealed with the jade ladle-shaped seal of the Xuanhe period. There are also labels on a slip of paper the width of one finger with a line of black characters alongside impressed by a wooden seal; these are the signatures of the craftsmen who mounted the calligraphy or paintings. Here, also, genuine and false are mixed together because at the time copies by skilled artists were inscribed as being genuine works. By the time of the Mingchang period (1190–1195) of the Jin dynasty (1115–1234) this practice was even more widespread. Nowadays, even though one may "buy a Wang (Xizhi) but get a Yang (Xin)[1]", they are not bad nevertheless.

Academy Paintings

The painters of the Song Painting Academy had first to present a draft before proceeding to a true final version. Landscapes, figures, flowers and trees, and birds and beasts are all unsigned; the same applies today to the Palace Manufactory paintings of Buddhist ceremonies and images. They are a dazzling sight and wondrous too. People today see an unsigned painting and immediately add a signature and inscription on the basis of its appearance and then seek to sell it for a high price: if it's a water buffalo then it's by Dai Song or a horse and it's by Han Gan. This is really laughable.

Single Strip

This form did not exist in the paintings of the Song and Yuan dynasties. Today, however, it is popular and people like them. Hung in a studio the vulgarity offends the eye and even if they are genuine they lose value.

Prominent Calligraphers and Painters

One should not be too indiscriminate in the collection of the calligraphy and paintings of the famous. Large items may be hung on studio walls and smaller items such as scrolls and albums may be placed on tables, but veritable antiques such as the works of Zhong Yao, Zhang Zhi (?–192), Wei Guan (220–291), Suo Jing (239–303), Gu Kaizhi, Lu Tanwei, Wu Daozi, Zhang Sengyou, together with lesser known historical figures, cannot be discussed in detail.

Famous calligraphers include: Wang Xizhi, Wang Xianzhi (344–386), Zhi Yong (dates unknown), Yu Shinan (558–638), Chu Suiliang (596–658 or 659), Ouyang Xun (557–641), Tang Emperor Xuanzong (685–762), Huai Su (737–799), Yan Zhenqing (708–784), Liu Gongquan (778–865), Zhang Xu, Li Huailin (dates unknown), Song Emperor Gaozong (1107–1187), Li Jianzhong (945–1013), Su Shi, Su Zhe (1039–1112), Mi Fu, Mi Youren, Fan Zhongyan (989–1052), Huang Tingjian (1045–1105), Cai Xiang (1012–1067), Su Shunqin (1008–1049), Huang Bosi (1079–1118), Xue Shaopeng (dates unknown), Fan Chengda (1126–1193), Zhang Jizhi (1186–1263), Wen Tianxiang (1236–1283), Zhao Mengfu, Xianyu Shu (1256–1301), Kang Lizishan (1295–1345), Zhang Yu (1238–1350), Ni Zan, Yang Weizhen (1296–1370), Ke Jiusi (1290–1343), Yuan Jue

(1266–1327) and Wei Su (1303–1372); in this dynasty there are Song Lian (1310–1381), Song Sui (1344–1380), Fang Xiaoru (1357–1402), Song Ke (1327–1387), Shen Du (1357–1434), Yu He (1307–1382), Xu Youzhen (1407–1472), Jin Cong (1449–1501), Shen Can (1357–1434), Xie Jin (1369–1415), Qian Pu (1408–1488), Sang Yue (1447–1513), Zhu Yunming (1460–1526), Wu Kuan (1435–1504), Wen Zhengming, Wang Chong (1494–1533), Li Yingzhen (1431–1493), Wang Ao (1450–1524), Tang Yin, Gu Lin (1476–1545), Feng Fang (1492–1563), Wen Peng (1498–1573), Wen Jia, Wang Guxiang (1501–1568), Lu Shen (1477–1544), Peng Nian (1505–1566), Lu Shidao (1511–1574), Chen Liu (1508–1575), Cai Yu (?–1541), Chen Chun (1483–1544), Zhang Fengyi (1527–1613), Wang Zhideng (1535–1612), Zhou Tianqiu (1514–1595), Xing Tong (1551–1612), and Dong Qichang. There are also Chen Bi (dates unknown) and Jiang Ligang (1444–1499), who are very well-known despite a lingering flavor of the Painting Academy.

Well-known artists include: Wang Wei, Li Sixun and Li Zhaodao, Zhou Fang, Guan Tong, Jing Hao (dates unknown), Dong Yuan, Li Cheng, Guo Xi, Mi Fu, Song Emperor Huizong, Mi Youren, Cui Bai (dates unknown), Huang Quan, Huang Jucai, Wen Tong (1018–1079), Li Gonglin (1049–1106), Guo Zhongshu (?–977), Dong Yu (dates unknown), Su Shi, Su Guo (1072–1123), Wang Shen (1048–1104), Zhang Shunmin (dates unknown), Yang Wujiu (1097–1169), Yang Jiheng (dates unknown), Chen Rong (dates unknown), Li Tang (1066–1150), Zhao Boju (?–c. 1173), Ma Yuan, Ma Kui (dates unknown), Xia Gui, Fan Kuan, Chen Jue (dates unknown), Chen Zhongmei (dates unknown), Li Shan (dates unknown),

---

1 Yang Xin (370–442) was a noted Southern Song dynasty calligrapher and nephew, pupil and artistic heir of Wang Xizhi. To have bought the nephew's work in the belief that it was the work of his uncle was a bargain nevertheless.

Fig. 83 *Pheasants Perched upon an Aragonite Rock*
Silk tapestry (Song dynasty)
Height 160.2 cm × Width 100.9 cm
Palace Museum, Taibei

Kesi is a traditional Chinese tapestry technique in which different colored threads are weft woven into different areas of the tapestry to produce richness of color. The colors on both sides of the tapestry are the same though the images are reversed. In this tapestry the colors are applied to a pale blue ground. A pair of golden pheasants disport themselves on a lake-rock with various kinds of flowers growing beside it. The effect is three-dimensional and the variations in color are both rich and exquisite.

Zhao Mengfu, Guan Daosheng (1262–1319), Zhao Yong (1289–c. 1361), Li Kan (1245–1320), Wu Zhen (1280–1354), Qian Xuan (c. 1239–c. 1300), Sheng Zizhao, Lu Guang (dates unknown), Cao Zhibai (1272–1355), Tang Di (dates unknown), Gao Shian (dates unknown), Gao Kegong (1248–1310), Wang Meng, Huang Gongwang, Ni Zan, Ke Jiusi, Fang Congyi (c. 1302–1393), Wang Mian (1287–1359), Dai Jin (1388–1462), Wang Fu (1362–1416), Xia Chang (1388–1470), Zhao Yuan (?–1376), Chen Ruyan (dates unknown), Xu Ben (1335–1393), Zhang Yu (1333–1385), Song Ke, Zhou Chen (dates unknown), Shen Zhenji (1400–?), Shen Hengji (1409–1477), Shen Zhou, Du Qiong (1396–1474), Liu Jue (1410–1472), Wen Zhengming, Wen Jia, Wen Boren (1502–1575), Tang Yin, Zhang Ling (dates unknown), Zhou Guan (dates unknown), Xie Shichen (1488–?), Chen Chun, Qiu Ying, Qian Gu (1508–?) and Lu Zhi (1496–1576). All these are well-known and indispensable to any collection. Any others are not collectable and should not be displayed even if they are part of a collection. Yet others, such as Zheng Dianxian, Zhang Fu, Zhong Li, Jiang Song (all of unknown dates), together with Zhang Lu (1464–1538 or 1537) and Wang Zhao (dates unknown) represent artistic heresy and are even less worthy of appreciation.

Song Embroidery and Silk Tapestry (*Kesi*)

Song embroideries are executed with a fine needle and thread and are exquisitely colored with a brilliance that strikes the eye. Landscapes differentiate between near and far, and buildings and pavilions appear remote and mysterious. Figures are vivid and lifelike, flowers are charming and birds peck and gobble. One should collect one or two examples as representatives of a form of painting (fig. 83).

Mounting

Autumn is the best time for mounting calligraphy and painting, then spring. The worst time is summer. Mounting cannot be undertaken in the damp heat of high summer or in freezing weather. Treated paper (paper treated with alum glue and wax) should not be used as the back will wrinkle. It is best to use large sheets of smooth untreated paper. Joins in the lining paper should avoid the faces of figures or other joins of painting paper. Moreover, if paper and lining joins coincide they will cause damage when rolling and unrolling. Joins should be serrated to distribute strength evenly. If they are too stiff, they will be too strong and if too slight, they will be weak. Dark colored mounting silk should not be burnished with a stone. Where ancient paintings have acquired a layer of dust over the years they should be soaked in a soap bean solution for several days and then laid on a flat table and the dirt scraped off. The painting will then appear bright and the colors unfaded. Paintings and calligraphy may be patched with a lining of oiled paper, the edges straightened and the gaps closed, the warp and weft straightened, the shape corrected, the losses repaired, thick and thin adjusted and all cleaned and stabilized. The generality of paintings, calligraphy and calligraphy copybooks should not be remounted as long as they remain intact; once they are remounted they immediately lose some of their vitality. The thickness of ancient paper should never be reduced.

Recipe for Making Paste

Mix one *jin* (about 500 g) of flour in an earthenware jar full of water and let it float and sink for a period of five days in the summer and ten in winter, judging it by one's sense of smell; soak half a *liang* (about 18 g) of *baiji* (*Bletilla striata*) in fresh water and add it, with three *fen* (about 1 g) of alum, to the original mixture to clear the dregs and then beat to a lump. Change and heat the water, pour away the water and place in a receptacle and wait until cool. Change the water daily and continue to soak. When about to use, add hot water. Never use thick paste or a worn brush.

The Correct Method of Mounting Calligraphy and Paintings as a Scroll

When mounting calligraphy and paintings as a scroll, the "heaven" and "earth" sections at the top and bottom of the scroll should be formed of black silk twill with a pattern of dragons and phoenix, clouds and cranes. Flower roundels and pale onion green or moonlight blue should not be used. The two hanging tapes (stave strips) of white twill of about one *cun* (about 3 cm) in width and the black silk border above and below the heart of the scroll, together with the white twill boss ends of the roller, should also use this pattern. Small paintings and pieces of calligraphy should be embedded in a pale moonlight blue silk backing with a golden yellow twill strip above, of the width of about half a *cun* (about 1.5 cm), and where there is an inscription there should be an embedded border the color of agarwood. This is the Xuanhe mounting method of the Song Emperor Huizong.

With large paintings and calligraphy, white twill may be used on all four edges though an embedded border is also permissible. Where the inscription panel inserted above the picture contains ancient commentaries or remarks, they should not be cut out; where there is no commentary they should be removed. There is no need for an embedded border on tall scrolls, though a delicate silk may be used for mounting according to the size of the calligraphy or picture. The "head leader" (*yinshou*) at the start of a hand scroll should be made of light or white Song letter paper, or Song, Jin (1115–1234) or Yuan letter paper decorated in gold. Korean cocoon paper and Japanese picture paper may also be used. In large scrolls the upper head leader measures five *cun* (about 15 cm) and the lower four *cun* (about 12 cm); in small scrolls the upper head leader measures four *cun* (about 12 cm) and the lower three *cun* (about 9 cm); the upper mounting excluding the roller should be just two *chi* in height (about 66 cm) and the lower mounting excluding the roller should be just one *chi* five *cun* in height (about 50 cm). Where a hand scroll measures two *chi* (about 66 cm) in length the head leader should be five *cun* (about 15 cm) in width with a front mounting of one *chi* (about 33 cm). I always use these measurements (ratios) as standard (fig. 84).

Fig. 84   Basic Layout for Scroll Mounting

horn, all decorated in the old fashion may be used but not red sandalwood (*zitan*), rosewood (*huali*) or cloisonné. Where the scroll is small and has roller knobs, they may be inlaid with precious jade. A roller knob is essential. It should not be a flat surface. Slips may be made of rhinoceros horn or jade. I once saw a Song jade slip half embedded in a brocade band: a true wonder.

Brocade Mounting

In ancient times there were brocades patterned with *chupu* (a design based on ancient oval-shaped gambling dice), pavilions, purple Bactrian camels, the Vermilion Bird, the two kinds of phoenix, ambulatory dragons and geese, all imperial creatures; there were also brocades patterned with hippocampus and turtles, and twills with grain and ball patterns, all Song dynasty products of the Xuanhe period. There are also Song embroideries of flowers-and-birds and landscapes used in mounting the head (upper part) of scrolls, all very antique. The still fashionable "petals on water" patterned brocade may also be used. However, Song satin or white ramie may not be used. Ribbons may be made of Song brocade.

Scroll Rollers

The ancients used carved sandalwood (*Santalum album*) as rollers for scrolls, decorated with gold or gilded, or with white jade, amber, agate or crystal: altogether a precious sight. Moreover, the fragrance of sandalwood repels insects and to choose it for making rollers is a decision of great significance. Today it is no longer possible to make rollers in the ancient way. They can only be made with the wood of the China fir tree. Rhinoceros horn may also be used (Editor's note: China began to use and develop rhinoceros horn in the distant past and articles of rhinoceros horn were a valued court tribute item. The rhinoceros appears frequently in ancient Chinese medicine manuals and the horn was much used. Water buffalo horn is now used instead). Ivory [Editor's note: obtained through overseas trade by Zheng He (1371?–1433) on his seven voyages to the Western Ocean during the early Ming dynasty] and ox

Storing Paintings

Paintings should be stored in boxes made of the wood of the China fir tree. On no account should the interior of the box be lacquered or papered for fear of causing damp. Each painting should be unrolled and examined in the fourth or fifth months and briefly exposed to sunlight and then returned to a box removed from the ground at a height of at least a *zhang* (about three meters) in order to avoid mold. When hung or displayed they should be changed after three to five days so that they do not weary the eye or become damp and dirty. Both sides of paintings or calligraphy should be brushed to remove dust and dirt and avoid damage to the painting before putting away.

Small Scroll Boxes

Boxes for small scrolls should be made so that they open laterally and the scroll can be inserted with a label giving the details, pasted on the scroll roller knob, thus making viewing extremely convenient.

Rolling up Scrolls

When rolling up scrolls, attention should be paid to leveling the edges. The scroll should not be too tight or too loose, nor should it be forcefully rolled up lest the silk tear. It may be brushed lightly with a piece of soft silk and it should not be viewed propped over one's hand: this will damage it.

Rubbings of Calligraphy

Historical examples carved on stone of the calligraphy of the great masters begin with the *Model Calligraphy of the Chunhua Era*, engraved by the Song Hanlin Academician and Court Calligrapher Wang Zhu (c. 928–969), which has an inscription in seal characters at the end. There are also *Rubbings from the Taiqing Pavilion* copied by imperial order by Cai Jing (1047–1126), *The Tanzhou Rubbings* copied by Shi Xibai (dates unknown), *The Jiangzhou Rubbings* copied by Secretarial Court Gentleman Pan Sidan (dates unknown), *The Ruzhou Rubbings* copied by Wang Cai (dates unknown) when he was governor of Ruzhou (in present day Henan), *Rubbings of the Two Wangs Father and Son* (Wang Xizhi and Wang Xianzhi) carved by Supervisor

Xu of the Song dynasty in Linjiang (now in Nanchang Municipality Jiangxi Province), rubbings from the Yuanyou period (1086–1094) of the Song dynasty known as *Further Rubbings from the Secret Chamber*, as well as rubbings from the Chunxi period (1174–1189) known as *Inner Office for Repairs Copy*. Original examples of Jin and Tang calligraphy made under the Song Emperor Gaozong include a reengraving of the *Model Calligraphy of the Chunhua Era* under the title *Further Rubbings from the Chunxi Secret Chamber*, the *Shengyuan Period Rubbings* that predate the Chunhua period (976–997) and were engraved by Xu Xuan (917–992) on the orders of Li Yu (937–978) the final ruler of the Southern Tang dynasty, the Song dynasty copy of the *Model Calligraphy of the Chunhua Era* made by Liu Cizhuang (dates unknown), without the date in seal characters and an added interpretive inscription, known as the *Rubbings from the Hall of the Performing Fish*, a recopy of the *Jiangzhou Rubbings* by Wu Gangjun known as the *Wugang Rubbings*, the Shangcai copy of the *Jiangzhou Rubbings* known as the *Caizhou Rubbings*, the *Rubbings from the Pavilion of Stars and Phoenix* engraved at Nankang (present day Ganzhou Municipality in Jiangxi Province) in the Song dynasty by Cao Yanyue (1157–1228), the *Jiaxiu Hall Rubbings* engraved by Li of Lujiang, the *Qianjiang Rubbings* engraved by Qin Shizhang (dates unknown) a native of Qian (in present day Guizhou Province), the recopy of the *Model Calligraphy of the Chunhua Era* made by the magistrate of Quanzhou in the Hongwu period (1371) of this (Ming) dynasty and known as the *Quanzhou Rubbings*, the collection engraved by Han Pingyuan (dates unknown) of the Song dynasty known as *Rubbings from the Hall of Jades*, the *Family School Rubbings* engraved by Xue Shaopeng, the reengraved *Rubbings from the Precious Jin Studio* by Cao Zhige (dates unknown), the *Rubbings from the Snow Stream Hall* engraved by Wang Tingyun (1156–1202), and the collection known as *Rubbings from the East Calligraphy Hall* engraved by Zhu Youdun (1379–1439), Prince of Zhou of this (Ming) dynasty. My own family engravings are *Rubbings from the Cloud Stopping Pavilion* and *Rubbings from the Lesser Cloud Stopping Pavilion*. There is also this dynasty's *Rubbings from the Studio of True Reward* by Hua Xia (dates unknown). All these are well-known block printed copies of rubbings cut with great skill and delicacy.

No collection can be without examples of seal script from the Zhou (1046–256 BC), Qin (221–206 BC), and Han dynasties as recorded in the *Stone Drum Texts* and the Tanshan Mountain Stone Inscriptions (in Hebei Province); the stone tablet inscriptions in seal script of Emperor Qinshihuang's chief minister Li Si (?–208 BC) at Taishan Mountain, Qushan Mountain and Yishan Mountain in the *Qin Oaths (Oaths of Chu)*, the eight lines of cursive script from the fragment of the *Thousand Character Classic*, Cai Yong's (133–192) *Xiacheng Tablet, Memorial Tablet for Guo Youdao (the Virtuous Guo), Jiuyi Hill Tablet, Tablet for Bian Shao, Tablet for Xuan Fu (Confucius)*, and *Beiyue Tablet*; the Later Han dynasty (25–220) Cui Ai's (77–142) *Tomb Tablet for Zhang Pingzi*; Guo Xiangcha's (dates unknown) clerical script inscriptions on the *Xiyue Huashan Mountain Tablet* and *Tablet for Governor Zhou Zhu*. Amongst rubbings from the Wei dynasty are Zhong Yao's *Memorial of Congratulation, Celebratory Tablet, Introduction of Ji Zhi, Abdication Tablet, Tablet of Encouragement* and *Tablet of Nobility*. Amongst rubbings from the state of Wu there is the *Guoshan Tablet* (present day Yixing in Jiangsu Province). Jin dynasty rubbings include *Record of the Orchid Pavilion, Fundamentals of Calligraphy, The Yellow Court Classic, Sacred Prefaces, Expeditions of General Yue Yi, In Praise of Dongfang Shuo, Poems of the Spirit of the Luo River, Tablet in Praise of Cao E, Statement of Pledge, Sheshan Temple Tablet, Pei Xiong Tablet, Xingfu Temple Tablet* (now one of the tablets in the Xi'an Forest of Steles), *Rubbing of Pledges, Tomb Inscription of the General for Pacifying the West, Liang Sichu Tablet, Tablet for Yang Hu* and the *Xianshan Mountain Tablet*, and Suo Jing's *Ode on War*. Amongst famous rubbings from the Song, Qi (479–502), Liang (502–557) and

Chen (557–589) dynasties are: *Tablet of the Sacred Words of Song Emperor Wendi*, Ni Gui's (dates unknown) *Golden Court Tablet*, the Liang dynasty calligrapher Xiao Ziyun's (487–549) *zhangcao* script (predecessor of cursive script) inscriptions of the *Ode on War, Mao Jun Tablet*, and *Epitaph for a Buried Crane*, Liu Ling's (dates unknown) *Tablet of Tears for Yang Hu*, the Chen dynasty calligrapher Zhi Yong's *Thousand Character Classic in Two Scripts* and *Cursive Script Orchid Pavilion Preface*. Amongst the well-known rubbings of the Northern Wei (386–534), Northern Qi (550–577) and Northern Zhou (557–581) dynasties are the Northern Wei dynasty Liu Xuanming's (dates unknown) *Mt Hua Temple Tablet*, Pei Sishun's (dates unknown) *Sutra of the Last Teachings of the Buddha*; the Northern Qi dynasty Wang Sicheng's (dates unknown) *Mengshan Tablet in the Eight Point Script, Nanyang Temple Clerical Script Tablet* and *Tianzhu Mountain Inscription*; and the Later Zhou dynasty (951–960) *Minister of Rites Tang Jing Tablet*. Well-known Sui dynasty rubbings include the *Kaihuang Era Orchid Pavilion Preface*, Xue Daoheng's (540–609) *Tablet for Erzhu Chang, Stupa Inscription*, and *Tablet at the Longcang Temple*. Tang dynasty rubbings include examples of Ouyang Xun's calligraphy in the *Jiucheng Palace Inscription, Tomb Tablet of Duke Fang Yanqian, Huadu Temple Stupa Inscription, Tablet for Lord Huangfu (Huangfu Dan), Tablet for Duke Wen Yanbo, Small Regular Script Thousand Character Classic, Heart Sutra, Tablet of Confucius' Dream of Retribution* and *Oath of Friendship Tablet*. Examples of Yu Shinan's calligraphy can be found in the *Confucius Family Temple Tablet, Discourse against Heresy, Baotan Tower Inscription, Yinsheng Buddhist Tablet, Epitaph for the Princess Ru'nan* and *Tablet of the Buddhist Master Meng*. Chu Suiliang's calligraphy can be found in his copy of the *Expeditions of General Yue Yi, Funeral Ode for the Tang Emperor Taizong, In Praise of Images of Loyal Worthies, In Praise of Dragons and Horses, Copy of the Orchid Pavilion Preface, Copy of the Sacred Prefaces, The Yellow Emperor's Classic of Stratagem* and the *Classic of Transformation*.

Liu Gongquan's calligraphy can be found in the *Diamond Sutra* and *Secret Tower Inscription in Memory of Master Da Da*. Yan Zhenqing's calligraphy can be found in the *Disputed Order of Precedence, Record of the Maiden Immortal Ma Gu, Eulogies in Memory of His Uncle and Nephew, Ancestral Temple Tablet, Memorial Tablet for Yuan Jie, Duobao Temple Tablet, Tablet of the Pool of Merciful Release, Record of the Archery Hall, Beiyue Temple Tablet, Cursive Script Thousand Character Classic, Cliff Tablet on the An Lushan Rebellion* and the *Gan Lu Model Calligraphy*. Huai Su's can be found in *An Account of My Life* (three versions), *Cursive Script Thousand Character Classic, Story of the Fairy of Dongling* and *Cang Zhen (Huai Su) and Duke Lu —Two Rubbings*. Li Yong's (678–747) can be found in *Yellow Emperor's Classic of Stratagem, Bodhi Tree Tablet, Tablet in Praise of Cao E, Qinwang Mountain Tablet, Tablet for General Zang Huailiang, Tablet in Memory of the Ye Youdao, Yuelu Temple Tablet, Kaiyuan Temple Tablet, Journey to Jingmen, Tablet for Li Sixun,* and *Ordination Platform Tablet*. Examples of the calligraphy of the Tang Emperor Taizong include *Epitaph Tablet for Wei Zheng* and *Rubbing of the Emperor Taizong's Cursive Script Inscription on the Vicissitudes of the Previous Dynasty*. The Tang Emperor Gaozong's (628–683) work includes *Epitaph Tablet for Li Ji*. Tang Emperor Xuanzong's examples include *Stupa Inscription for Master Yi Xing*, the *Classic of Filial Piety* and *Tablet for Princess Jin Xian*. Sun Guoting (646–691) wrote *Discourse on Calligraphy*. Tang dynasty tablets also include: *Two Tablets for Ji Zi of Yan Ling*; Liu Gongchuo's (763–832) *Tablet for the Zhuge Family Temple*; Li Yangbing's (dates unknown) *Thousand Character Classic in Seal Characters, Confucius Temple Tablet* and *Chenghuang Temple Tablet*; Ouyang Tong's (?–691) *Zen Master Daoyin's Tablet*; Xue Ji's (649–713) *Tablet of the Immortal Ascent of the Prince*; Zhang Xu's *Cursive Script Thousand Character Classic*, and the Buddhist monk Xingdun's (dates unknown) *Sutra of the Last Teachings of the Buddha*. In the Southern Tang dynasty there was Yang Yuanding's (dates unknown) *Ziyang Temple Tablet* and in the Song dynasty the works of Huang Tingjian and Su Shi, such as the poems *Garden Pools of Yangzhou* and *Heavenly Horses*. There was Zhao Mengfu from the Yuan dynasty and Song Ke (dates unknown) and Song Guang (dates unknown) in this (Ming) dynasty whose fine calligraphy should be collected and appreciated but not in too untidy and indiscriminate a fashion.

Paper and Ink of North and South

The patterning of the ancient paper of the north ran horizontally and the texture was thick and rather loose and did not absorb ink well. Northern ink (made mostly with pine smoke) is a light greenish/black in color and does not blend well with wax. Consequently, rubbings made with northern ink are wrinkled and insipid (rather like light cloud crossing a dark sky), hence they are called "cicada wing rubbings." In southern part, the patterning of paper is vertical and the ink is made from lampblack and candle wax so that rubbings from the south are a pure gleaming black and are called "raven's gold rubbings."

Distinguishing Old and New Rubbings

Ancient rubbings have a long history and have been remounted many times. Their ink is thick and as dense as fresh lacquer, the paper gleams as if burnished and shows no sign of the ink bleeding. Moreover, the ink also gives off a mysterious fragrance.

Mounting Rubbings

Ancient rubbings should use a board of suitable wood of a thickness of about one *fen* (about 0.3 cm) upon which is incised the number of rolls. Not quite so good is a wood of a thickness of about five *fen* (about 1.5 cm). This may be covered with antique-colored brocade or brocade bearing a blue-and-white pattern. Twill or mixed colors may not be used. Boxes should be made for storage and should be roughly square and not long and narrow. They may have borders of white deer paper (a superior paper for calligraphy and painting requiring advanced skills in the difficult manufacturing process). Silk may not be used for borders. Ten volumes to a box; it is best if the boxes are all of the same size.

Song Dynasty Woodblock Printed Copybooks

In collecting calligraphy, Song dynasty wood block printed copybooks are valued, the carving of the thick and thin brushstrokes is balanced and regular and good examples include the calligraphy of Ouyang Xun and Liu Gongquan. The paper quality is clean and even and the ink smooth and clear; a single line frames the text and although detection of the frequent avoidance of taboo characters (such as the emperor's name) is part of proving provenance, it is not decisive (fig. 85). The best calligraphy examples are drawn from Ban Gu's (32–92) *History of the Han* and Fan Ye's (398–445) *History of the Later Han* together with *Zuo's Commentary on the Spring and Autumn Annals*, *Sayings of the States*, *Laozi*, *Zhuangzi*, *Records of the Historian*, *Selections of Refined Literature* and the works of the Hundred Schools of Thought. The remaining poetry and writings of the well-known, miscellaneous records and Daoist and Buddhist works are secondary. Fresh printings with new blocks on white bark paper are the best; binding liners of paper made from bamboo are acceptable. Books with backing paper that is overwritten with comments or notes should not be collected.

Hanging Paintings According to the Season

On the first day of the (Lunar) New Year one should hang Song paintings of the gods of good fortune and ancient sages. On either side of

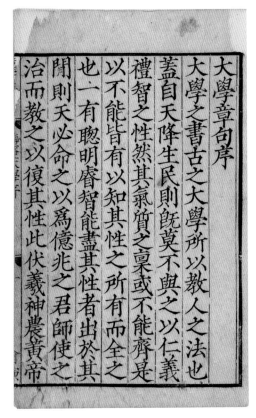

Fig. 85   Song Dynasty Woodblock Print

Very few examples survive from the flourishing woodblock printing industry of the Song dynasty. Song dynasty woodblock printers used fine textured but tough paper, a spacious elegant format and typefaces that differed in style from place to place. The ink used was a pure, even black with almost the aesthetic appeal of calligraphy.

the fifteenth day (Lantern Festival) one should hang paintings of lantern viewing and puppet shows. During the first and second months one should hang paintings of spring outings, court ladies, plum blossom, the blossoms of apricot, camellia, magnolia, and peach; on the third day of the third month one should hang Song paintings of Xuanwu, the God of the North; before and after the Qingming Festival one should display paintings of tree peonies and herbaceous peonies; on the eighth day of the fourth month Song and Yuan paintings and embroidered images of the Buddha should be displayed; on the fourteenth day of the fourth month, the birthday of Lu Dongbin (a Daoist sage), his image should be displayed; on the fifth day of the fifth month (Duanwu, a day when negative influences are at their height)

Fig. 86 *Praying for Skill*
(detail)

Anon. (Five dynasties or
Northern Song dynasty)
Ink and color on silk
Height 161.6 cm ×
Width 110.8 cm
Metropolitan Museum of
Art, New York

The prayer for skill was
a Chinese folk custom
in which girls assembled
in the courtyard on the
seventh night of the
seventh lunar month
to pray for knowledge
and skill from the
Weaver Girl in the stars.
This painting depicts a
group of palace maids
gathering to seek the
Weaver Girl's help. The
black table is set with a large number of bowls, all of the
same size, used for the ceremony of "casting a needle
to seek skill." After having been heated in the sun the
water in the bowls forms a film of microorganisms on
the surface upon which a needle is carefully placed. The
shadow that it throws on the bottom of the bowl is then
examined. If the shadow takes the form of a weaver's
shuttle it signifies that the Weaver Girl in the heavens will
grant the maid's wish.

and as protection against disaster there should
be displays of Daoist talismans and scenes
from the Duanwu Festival, dragon boats, tiger
shaped artemesia leaves and depictions of
toads, lizards, snakes, spiders and centipedes
(the "five poisons"), all by the hand of masters
of the Song and Yuan dynasties; during the
sixth month, there should be cooling displays
of large landscapes, pavilions and buildings,
dense misty trees and rocks, large depictions
of clouds and mountains, lotus picking and
escaping the summer heat; on the evening of
the seventh day of the seventh month (Festival
of the Cowherd and Weaver Girl) one should
display paintings of needle threading by the
light of the moon (fig. 86), the weaver girl
star (Vega), buildings and pavilions, banana
leaves, and court ladies; during the eighth
month paintings of ancient osmanthus trees,
flowers, and book rooms; during the ninth
and tenth month chrysanthemum, hibiscus,
rivers and hills in autumn, forests of maple; in
the eleventh month snowscapes, wintersweet,
narcissus and camellia; and in the twelfth
month images of the demon repeller Zhong
Kui, together with paintings of welcome to
good fortune, the expulsion of demons and
Zhong Kui marries off his sister; on the 25th of
the first month paintings of the Jade Emperor,
immortals in cloud carriages of many colors;
on the occasion of moving house one should

display paintings of the Daoist master Ge
Hong moving his habitation and so forth; at
celebrations of longevity one should display
paintings of the God of Longevity and the
Queen Mother of the West from the Painting
Academy; when praying for fine weather it is
the sun god Dong Jun and when praying for
rain it is ancient paintings of wind and rain
and sacred dragons and thunder awakening
the spring; the Beginning of Spring (first of
the Twenty-Four Solar Terms dividing the year
into periods) is marked by hanging images of
Tai Yi and the Emperor of the East (both gods
that have charge of spring). All hung according
to the season and to mark the passage of the
different times of the year. However, large
paintings of gods, swallows and apricots, plum
blossom bed curtains, plum blossom on walls,
pines and cypress, cranes and deer are in poor
taste and should not be hung. Small scenes
from the Song and Yuan dynasties, ancient
trees and bamboo and rocks are not part of the
theory of the sequence of seasons.

CHAPTER SIX
TABLES AND COUCHES

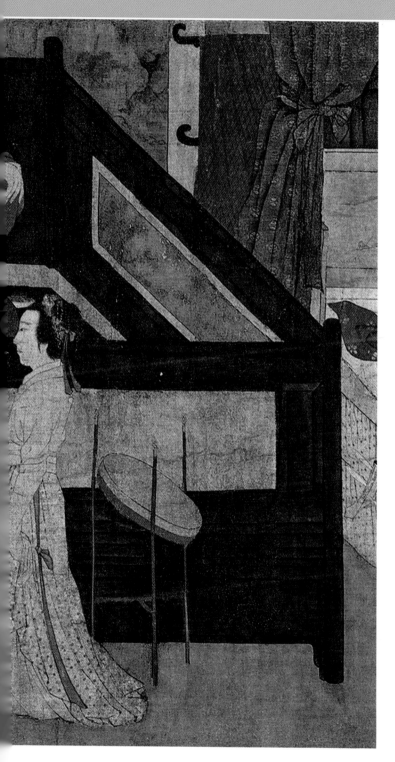

Despite differences in the dimensions of the small tables and couches made by the ancients, once placed in a room or studio they appear elegant and attractive and extremely convenient whether for sitting, reclining or lying down. When entertaining guests after a banquet they may be used for the display of sutras and histories, the perusal of calligraphy and paintings, the exhibition of bronze tripods and sacrificial vessels as well as for the laying out of refreshments and the placing of mats and pillows. Nothing is impossible. Those made today are ornamented and carved to appeal to the vulgar eye, those of ancient manufacture have disappeared and that is a matter of deep regret.

Fig. 87 *Chancellor Han Xizai's Evening Banquet* (detail)
Gu Hongzhong (Five dynasties)
Ink and color on silk
Height 28.7 cm × Length 335.5 cm
Palace Museum, Beijing

This scroll reproduces historical scenes from Chancellor Han Xizai's entertainment of guests at his evening banquets. Numerous examples of the domestic furniture of the time appear in the painting; Luohan couches, tables and flat topped tables, chairs with backrests and drum frames amongst others, all of them of a simple fluidity of design. We know of Wen Zhenheng's admiration for the design of ancient furniture from Shen Chunze's foreword to his book.

Couches

The standard dimensions and structure for couches are: height of base, one *chi* two *cun* (approximately 36 cm); height of backrest, one *chi* three *cun* (approximately 39 cm); length, just over seven *chi* (approximately 2.1 meters); width, three *chi* five *cun* (approximately 115 cm). The whole is surrounded by rails of wood inset with speckled bamboo, the feet should be steady with a backrest on three sides, the back and two sides the same. Some couches display ancient crackle decoration, others from the Yuan dynasty are inlaid with mother-of-pearl①. These are naturally elegantly shaped. Examples with just four individual feet[1] or feet made in the shape of praying mantis legs are to be avoided though a wooden support is permissible. Recently there have couches made with Dali marble inlay, others made of red or black polished lacquer carved with bamboo or trees filled with powder and yet others

① Mother-of-pearl inlay, made from seashells ground thin and used to decorate furniture and vessels to add to their attractiveness.

with inlays of new mother-of-pearl: all these completely lack elegance. However, those made according to the ancient style in the wood of the *huanan* tree (*Machilus pauhoi*), in red sandalwood, ebony (*Diospyros ebenum*) and rosewood, all these may be used but once extended or enlarged, though they may be pronounced beautiful, they are vulgar. I have also seen couches made in the Yuan dynasty with a length of one *zhang* five *chi* (approximately 4.5 meters) and breadth of over two *chi* (approximately 60 cm) and without any backrest as the ancients shared couches together for sleeping, feet to feet, heads at the opposite ends. Despite their elegant simplicity of structure, they are no longer in use (fig. 88).

Short Couches

Short couches have a height of about one *chi* (approximately 30 cm) and length of four *chi* (approximately 120 cm) and are placed in Buddha halls and studios where they may be used for contemplation and seated Zen or for discussing the Daoist mysteries. They are also well suited for reclining and are commonly known as Boddhisattva chairs.

Small Tables

Small side tables are made from the curved split halves of naturally crooked rare trees with three feet added from other branches. They

Fig. 88 Yellow Rosewood (*Huanghuali*) Couch
Late Ming/early Qing dynasty
Length 200.7 cm

A couch is a long, narrow and comparatively low bed-shaped piece of furniture used as seating. It is an indispensable item in the elegant life of the literati. In old paintings one often sees gentleman scholars seated on couches admiring antiques and exchanging notes. It is difficult to identify the kind of couch described by Wen Zhenheng from the examples that have survived, we can only glimpse a little of their design and decoration in the furniture of the Ming dynasty.

Fig. 89 *Xiao Yi Obtains a Copy of the Record of the Orchid Pavilion by Subterfuge* (Southern Song dynasty copy, detail)

Yan Liben
Ink and color on silk
Height 27 cm × Width 340 cm
Liaoning Provincial Museum

The painting depicts the story of the Investigating Censor Xiao Yi who, on the orders of the Tang Emperor Taizong, swindled the Buddhist monk Bian Cai out of his copy of the *Record of the Orchid Pavilion* in the hand of the great calligrapher Wang Xizhi. The painting shows Bian Cai seated on a high-backed rattan Zen chair. It is just possible to make out the pattern of veining in the rattan.

may be polished and placed on a couch or mat and one may rest one's head in the hand[2]. I have also seen illustrations of the ancients lying down and resting their feet on such a table. The form is elegantly odd.

Zen Chairs

Zen chairs are made from the rattan that grows on Tiantai Mountain or from the roots of old trees that twist like a dragon and grow outwards in all directions and from which gourd ladles, rain hats, prayer beads and bottles may be hung (fig. 89). They should be polished like jade and the best are those that bear no sign of axe or adze. I have recently seen such chairs over-decorated with *lingzhi* (fungus) designs in red, white, black, dark green and yellow.

Winged Tables

Winged tables should be made from fine textured wood such as rosewood, ironwood (*Mesua ferrea*) and fragrant *nanmu* (*Machilus odoratissima*). Although wide examples are considered the best, they should not exceed eight *chi* (approximately 240 cm) in length or a thickness of five *cun* (approximately 15 cm). The raised upturns at either end should not be sharp but rounded so as to be in the ancient style. There is a kind of Japanese natural table that has a foot stretcher beneath, extremely strange. It may not have four feet like a calligraphy table but may be supported by the roots of ancient trees or the feet may be made from wood. Provided the surface of the table is broad and thick and there is space, it may be carved with *ruyi* patterns and clouds but not with dragons and phoenix or flowers and plants: that would be vulgar. Recent examples, long and narrow, are abominable.

---

1 That is without a stretcher frame.
2 By placing the elbow on the table.

Desks

The surface of desks should be broad with an inlaid border of little over half a *cun* (about 1.5 cm) and with feet that are low and slender. This would be the ancient style. The vulgar models, long and narrow with rounded corners are not to be used. Lacquered desks are vulgar in the extreme (fig. 91).

Wall Tables

There are no limits on the dimensions of wall tables but they should not be too broad. Raised corners and flying clouds and praying mantis legs, these styles honor the Buddha. There are others in the old style such as those inlaid with

Fig. 90 *Scholarly Colloquy at the Western Garden* (detail)
Liu Songnian
Ink and color on silk
Height 34 cm × Length 191 cm
Palace Museum, Taibei

The painting depicts a gathering of eminent Song dynasty literati at the Western Garden. A number of scholars are gathered round a large square table, one of whom is writing a piece of calligraphy. An assortment of literary utensils covers the tabletop.

Fig. 91 Yellow Rosewood Desk or Writing Table
Late Ming dynasty
Height 94 cm × Width 94 cm × Depth 87 cm

The word *zhuo*, table, implies the existence of vertical height. The table's four legs are perpendicular to its four corners. There are a number of kinds of table; square, long, round, for wine, for playing the *qin* and for chess. The table illustrated is a comparatively typical desk in the style of the late Ming dynasty.

Dali marble and Qiyang stone which are also acceptable.

Square Tables

The best square tables are painted with old lacquer and should be broad and plain and large enough to seat a number of people and to display calligraphy and paintings (fig. 90). The recent "eight immortals" tables (which can only seat two people on each side) are only suitable for banquets and are by no means elegant pieces of furniture. Illustrations of small tables for leaning and resting against may be found elsewhere.

Platform Tables

Platform tables are made by the Japanese in various shapes and sizes, they are of great

Fig. 92 *A Gathering of Nine Old Friends* (detail)

Attributed to Li Gonglin
Ink line drawing on paper
Height 30.7 cm × Length 238 cm
Liaoning Provincial Museum

This drawing is based on the story of the meeting of the nine old friends, the poet Bai Juyi and eight guests, in the private gardens of his residence. The detail shows four of the old friends gathered round a table, participating in the enjoyment of looking at paintings or doing calligraphy. The chairs in which they are seated are typical of the Song dynasty and are of the "ancient style" advocated by Wen Zhenheng.

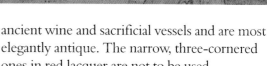

elegance and beauty. Some have gilded inlay at the four corners, others are inlaid with strips of gold and silver and others are incised with a hidden underglaze decoration (*anhua*). They fetch an extremely high price. There are some now made in the old style, some of which are excellent, that may be used for the display of ancient wine and sacrificial vessels and are most elegantly antique. The narrow, three-cornered ones in red lacquer are not to be used.

Chairs

Fig. 93 Yellow Rosewood Curved-Back Chairs
Ming dynasty
Height 100.7 cm × Width 59.6 cm × Depth 46.4 cm

Chairs did not exist in ancient China and up until the Tang dynasty people sat on mats on the ground. Foreign folding chairs (*jiaochuang*) were the earliest seats with height to be introduced into China. In the Tang dynasty, seats with backs and arms began to be known simply as chairs (*yizi*). From the Song dynasty onwards, furniture developed in shape from low to high. Seats in the form of chairs had already become a common piece of furniture in the homes of ordinary people and they subsequently developed into high- and low-backed chairs, ordinary folding chairs (*jiaoyi*) and curved-back chairs (*quanyi*) in various shapes and with various functions.

There are very many shapes of chair and I have seen Yuan dynasty chairs inlaid with mother-of-pearl, broad enough to seat two people and made in ancient form; the most valuable are made from ebony inlaid with Dali marble but the manufacture should be in ancient form. In sum, chairs should be low and not high, broad and not narrow (figs. 92, 93). As to the vulgar kinds of folding chairs with backrests, bamboo chairs from Wujiang (in present-day Jiangsu) and the Zen chairs produced in Zhuanzhu Street in Suzhou, they are in no way to be used. Chair feet should be capped with a bamboo border and will last for a long time.

A stool is a wooden seat without back or arms. The seating panel can be either square or round.

Stools

Stools have two shapes: square with four equal sides (fig. 94) and long that can accommodate two people. Round stools should be large with four everted feet. In ancient times there were also stools with mother-of-pearl inlay and of red or black lacquer, bamboo stools and those bound in silk cord, which are vulgar and should not be used.

Benches

Benches with inlaid borders are elegant; those with a center of Chinese weeping cypress (*Cupressus funebris*) and a border of ebony inlay are the most elegant. Alternatively, other woods may be used as well as those lacquered in black.

Folding Chairs

Folding chairs (fig. 95) or "barbarian beds" have the rounded wooden bars of the two feet inlaid and hinged with silver. They may be taken on mountain excursions or used on boats. They are extremely convenient. Folding chairs in gold lacquer are vulgar beyond use.

Cupboards and Cabinets

Cabinets for the storage of books must be able to hold many volumes, the larger and more elegant the better, but they must only have the depth of a single book though the width may exceed one *zhang* (about three meters). There must be two doors, not four or six. Small cabinets may be mounted on a stand for elegance. Four feet are rather vulgar, but if feet have to be used they should be a height of over one *chi* (about 30 cm). If a base is used beneath, it should only be two *chi* (about 60 cm) in height. Cabinets may also

Fig. 95 Yellow Rosewood Folding Chair with Arms
Ming dynasty
Height 94.8 cm

Folding chairs first appeared in the Tang dynasty and were a development of the so-called "barbarian bed", which gradually took shape from the Five dynasties onwards and appeared in large numbers during the Song dynasty. As it could be folded, carried, and stored it was extremely convenient. Following its appearance in the Song dynasty it became part of the impedimenta of officials and other distinguished personages.

be placed one upon another. Bases are best in the form of an open frame. Small cabinets are generally two *chi* (about 60 cm) square and suitable for the placing of ancient bronzes and small jades. Large cabinets made from China fir (*Cunninghamia lanceolota*) protect against book-eating insects. Small cabinets of speckled bamboo, *Phoebe zhennan*, mahogany and catalpa are particularly elegant. Black lacquer with a crackle pattern is a fine material and various other woods may be used, but true value lies in the lack of vulgarity. Cupronickel may not be used for hinge shanks. Use copper in the ancient fashion with both ends having the sharpness of a shuttle. It is best not to use nails. Bamboo cupboards and those with upright wooden bars are objects of the market place or medicine shop and are not to be used. There are small cabinets with Palace Manufactory incised and filled decorations on lacquer, and some made in Japan. They are all fine examples. Cabinets for the storage of Buddhist sutras should be lacquered in red, somewhat square in shape and a little deeper as sutras are comparatively long.

Fig. 96   Yellow Rosewood Bookcase
Ming dynasty
Height 175 cm × Width 79.5 cm × Depth 32 cm
The development of furniture in China reached its summit during the Ming dynasty. Based on the furniture of the previous dynasties, the furniture of the Ming dynasty developed unique aesthetic characteristics in material, construction, workmanship, and decoration that were concise but not simple. The illustration shows a relatively small bookcase typical of the Ming dynasty.

Bookcases

Bookcases are of two sizes, large and small, the large just over seven *chi* (about 2.1 m) high and twice that in width and containing 12 open compartments, each compartment holding ten volumes for ease of finding and taking out. The lowest compartments should not hold books because of the need to avoid damp due to closeness to the ground. The feet should be quite high. Small bookcases may be placed on top of low tables. Flat bookcases with two compartments, or cases made from squared timber and bamboo, and red or black lacquer cases do not bear use (fig. 96).

Fig. 97   *A Spring Outing Late to Return* (detail)
Anon. (Song dynasty)
Ink and color on Silk
Height 24.2 cm × Width 25.3 cm
Palace Museum, Taibei
The painting depicts an elderly man setting out on a spring outing on horseback. An escort of servants front and rear is seen carrying chairs and stools or using a shoulder pole. One servant carries an outdoor portable folding chair over his shoulder.

Buddha Cabinets and Tables

Buddha cabinets and tables should be made of red or black lacquer and should be of dignified appearance without any air of femininity. Those with carved decoration made at the Palace Manufactory, those with ancient crackle patterns and those made in Japan are all elegant pieces. There have recently been some put together using pieces with a crackle pattern. They may be used provided they are not vulgar. Eight-cornered and rounded-corner versions with new laquer, together with Buddha fired at the Dehua Kiln, absolutely cannot be used.

Beds

Small Song and Yuan dynasties' lacquer crackle-patterned beds are the best (fig. 98), next are the single beds made by the Palace Manufactory and then the beds made by skilled craftsmen. All these may be used. In Yongjia (in present-day Zhejiang Province) and eastern Yue (present-day Guangdong Province) there are folding beds convenient for use on boats. However, bamboo-canopied (*piaoyan*[1]) and elaborately roofed bed chambers, as well as brightly lacquered, swastika-patterned and key-patterned beds, are all vulgar. Recently there have been beds made of Chinese weeping cypress cut to the shape of slender bamboo, which are very delicate and suitable for women's quarters or a studio.

[1] Lit. "floating eaves," a canopy that extends over the steps to a bed.

Chests

There are chests made in Japan of black lacquer inlaid with gold and silver strips and more than one *chi* (about 30 cm) in depth. They have locks and hinges of great ingenuity, suitable for the storage of ancient jades and

Fig. 98 *Chancellor Han Xizai's Evening Banquet* (detail)

Historically speaking, the Song dynasty was one in which culture flourished and prospered and furniture making became highly developed. The black bed in the painting is typical of bedroom furniture in the Song dynasty.

treasure or small scrolls of the Jin and Tang dynasties. There is also another kind, not as large, of elegant appearance, light as paper and decorated with patterns of interlocking lozenges and tassels, which can be used for the storage of scrolls and perfumes and trinkets and that may be kept in a studio ready for use. There is a further kind with a crackle pattern, curved above and square below, in which the ancients stored sutras and that looks impressive when placed on a Buddhist altar.

Screens

The shape of screens is very ancient. Screens where the lower part has been delicately inlaid with Dali marble are the most valuable. Next are screens of Qiyang stone and then those of Huarui stone (*ophicalcite*) (from Luoyang in present day Henan Province). If old screens are unobtainable, new screens may be made in the old style. Screens of pasted paper, surround screens and screens of wood do not make the grade.

Footstools

Footstools (*gundeng*) are made from wood and have a length of two *chi* (about 60 cm) and a width of six *cun* (about 18 cm) and are of normal height (fig. 99). The surface consists of a grid with two spaces in which are mounted two wooden rollers that, when trodden backwards and forwards, massage the Yongquan point, the seat of energy in the soles of the feet, and provide marvelous exercise. Large square footrests of bamboo may also be used. Ancient narrow hollow bricks originally used for supporting a *qin* may be used in the summer as a cool footrest.

Fig. 99 Yellow Rosewood Footstool with Rollers
Ming dynasty
Height 21 cm × Width 77 cm × Depth 31.2 cm

The history of the footstool reached its apogee in the Ming dynasty when the health care of the time regarded the practice of putting the feet up as an integral part of good health, thus producing the footstool. Footstools were frequently placed beneath desks and painting tables or beside beds and couches so that the scholar, fatigued by study, could place his feet on the footstool and without the exertion of too much effort tread the rollers backwards and forwards to relieve fatigue, hence the name roller stool.

CHAPTER SEVEN
VESSELS AND UTENSILS

The ancients made vessels for their utility and did not begrudge the work required, hence their excellence, unlike the careless work that followed. From bells, sacrificial tripods, sabers, swords, dishes and *yi* (ancient gourd-shaped scoops for water) to paper and ink, all rejoiced in fine work and not merely engraved inscriptions or signatures. People today are of limited knowledge and being accustomed to the ordinary and everyday are thus unable to distinguish the elegant from the vulgar. There are others, in thrall to magnificence, who cannot perceive the elegance of antiquity and regard windows and tables as of no account, speaking grandly of display and arrangement. One simply cannot merely agree with them.

Fig. 100 *Enjoying Antiques in the Bamboo Court*
(detail)
Qiu Ying
Ink and color on silk
Height 41.4 cm × Width 33.8 cm
Palace Museum, Beijing

A number of gentleman scholars are gathered together in a bamboo court to assess the quality of antiques, calligraphy and paintings. The table is spread with antique bronzes and the literary utensils of the library.

Incense Burners

The tripods and sacrificial vessels of the Xia (2070–1600 BC), Shang and Zhou dynasties as well as those of the Qin and Han periods and the incense burners produced by the Guan, Ge (fig. 101), Ding, and Xuande kilns, are all items for appreciation by the connoisseur rather than for everyday use. The most suitable for actual use are the slightly large bronze burners and vessels of the Xuande reign. The incense burners cast by Jiang of the Yuan dynasty are also acceptable. However, one may not use burners designed for burning incense in front of images of the Buddha or the burners used by Daoists to produce the elixir of immortality, nor gilded or cupronickel tripod burners in the shape of fish or elephants. Most to be deprecated are the burners cast by Pan and Hu Wenming (dates unknown) of Yunjian (Songjiang in present-day Shanghai), vulgar burners decorated with the eight auspicious Buddhist objects, or scenes from Japan, or burners with a studded surface, or new porcelain products from the Jian Kiln, or porcelain burners in five colors. Dark green *boshan* bronze burners may sometimes be used. Tripod vessels of wood may be used in the

Fig. 101   Ge Kiln Gray Crackle Glaze Tripod Burner with Lugs
Song dynasty
Height overall 11.1 cm, diameter at mouth 12.4 cm
Palace Museum, Taibei

The Ge Kiln is one of the five great kilns of the Song dynasty. The remaining four are the Jun, Ru, Guan and Ding kilns. Crackle patterning is a particular characteristic of the Ge Kiln. The three-footed type is one of the most frequently encountered kinds of incense burner.

mountains, burners of stone may only be used in the service of Buddha, the remainder are of no worth. The tripods and sacrificial vessels of the ancients all had covers and bases. Today, people make them of wood, those of ebony being the finest though red sandalwood and rosewood are acceptable. Those with water caltrop or sunflower patterning are vulgar. The lid of the burner may take the form of a Song dynasty jade hat button or *luduan*[1] or sea animal provided that it matches the size of the burner. Ancient agate and crystal may also be used.

Incense Boxes

The best incense boxes are the Song dynasty

carved lacquer boxes the color of coral. In ancient times the best were boxes with a pommel scroll design, then designs of flowers and plants and last designs of figures. There are boxes lacquered in layers of five colors and incised both deep and shallow so that the different colors are revealed by the form of the box; those with red flowers and green leaves or black lacquer on yellow are not as good. There are Japanese boxes of three or five compartments and portable boxes decorated with gold and silver strips. There are large and small incense boxes manufactured by the Orchard Yard[①] where the lids and base were made in different workshops and in different colors, hence the value of those of a single color. The colored lacquer infill incense boxes produced by the Palace Manufactory may also be used. Small boxes include the "split sugar cane" and "bangle" types produced at the Ding and Rao (i.e. Jingdezhen Kiln in Jiangxi) kilns, the remainder are of no account. Particularly to be avoided are boxes with characters outlined or written in gold. The carved lacquer boxes produced in Huizhou and the porcelain boxes from the Xuande and Guan kilns of the Chenghua (1465–1487), Jiajing, and Longqing periods should not be used.

① Orchard Yard: an establishment set up in the Yongle reign of the Ming dynasty to manufacture lacquerware.

Incense Burner Covers

The fire within a burner may not be extinguished because incense does not burn with a flame. Its charm lies in the way it smoulders. It burns easily when dried out and this is called a "living fire." Earthenware shards are the best for separating off the fire, then bits of Ding Kiln porcelain followed by slivers of jade. Gold and silver should not be used. Using fireproof fabric the size of a cash[2] to surround the sides has wonderful results.

Fire Tongs

Copper fire tongs are the best, those made by Hu Wenming of Yunjian and those of cupronickel from the Southern Capital (Nanjing) may also be used. Silver and gold may not be used nor those with a raised pattern.

Tong Vases

The vases produced by the Guan, Ge and Ding kilns are all good but are not for everyday use. There are some of recent manufacture from the land of Wu with short necks and fine holes that because of the weight of the base will not topple over when tongs are inserted. Copper vases are of no account.

Sleeve Warmers

Sleeve warmers are indispensable for perfuming clothes and warming the hands. The Japanese-made warmers in the shape of a lacquer drum with a reticulated lid are the best. The two recent kinds, heavy and light and round and square, are of vulgar manufacture.

Hand Braziers

Hand braziers are made in the form of ancient bronze basins or grain vessels. The bronze drum tripod braziers with beast heads of the Xuande reign may also be used but not those of brass and cupronickel or red sandalwood or rosewood. Tripod braziers cast in ancient times have a pattern of drooping or raised lotus blossom in fine lines; box-shaped ones are the most elegant. The braziers in the shape of a pomander that are placed in bedding are vulgar and should be thrown away.

---

1 An auspicious mythical sacred polyglot animal resembling a unicorn with the body of a deer and capable of travelling very long distance in the space of a day.
2 Chinese copper coin come in strings.

Incense Stick Holders

Amongst old incense stick holders those made by Li Wenfu (dates unknown) with decorations of flowers-and-birds and stones and bamboo are valued for their antique simplicity. However, if they are overelaborate or carved with images of people or stories, then they are tasteless items and not to be placed in the bosom or sleeve.

Writing Brush Racks

Although brush racks were made in the ancient past, nowadays inkstones in the form of hills, such as those made of stone from Lingbi or Ying stone, with mountain ranges that rise and fall and that bear no sign of axe or chisel, are used. As a consequence, brush racks have been abandoned. There are ancient jades in the form of mountains (fig. 102) and old jade in the form of a mother cat with kittens, six or seven *cun* (about 20 cm) in length, the mother cat in white jade and the kittens represented in flawed jade or pure yellow or black tortoiseshell. There are ancient bronze brush racks comprising two gilded and burnished hornless dragons opposite each other; racks with spaces formed by twelve mountains and racks with

Fig. 102   Black Jade Brush Holder in the Form of a Mountain

Southern Song/Yuan dynasty
Height 4.4 cm × Length 16.7 cm × Depth 1.8 cm
Palace Museum, Taibei

This brush holder in the form of a mountain is made of blue-green jade and is carved to represent ranges of mountains, one behind the other. The concave depressions between the mountains make convenient resting places for brushes.

spaces formed from a single coiled hornless dragon. Fired kiln ware includes white triple mountains from the Ding Kiln as well as five mountains and a recumbent child amongst lotus blossom, all of which may be collected and enjoyed without the necessity of placing them on tables or amongst inkstones. The vulgar furnish themselves with old tree roots twisted into a myriad of shapes or in the form of dragons complete with claws. All of these are to be avoided and cannot be used.

Brush Rests

Brush rests are not much seen. In the ancient past they were gilded, about six or seven *cun* (about 20 cm) long, just over one *cun* two *fen* (about 3.6 cm) in height and over two *cun* in width (about 6 cm) and could accommodate four brushes. Those that resemble a brush rack

are ugly in the extreme and should be discarded even if they are of ancient form (fig. 103).

Screened Brush Holders

Screened brush holders are brush holders with an inlaid screen; they are not of elegant appearance. There are those, both square and round, made by the Song Palace Manufactory in decorated jade, as well as those of ancient Dali marble not above a *chi* (about 30 cm) square that set on a table are of loathsome appearance. It would be well to discard this kind.

Brush Pots

Brush pots (fig. 104) made of Hunan bamboo or palm wood are the best. Moso bamboo (*Phyllostachys edulis*) inlaid with ancient bronze is also good and red sandalwood, ebony and rosewood may be used from time to time, but pots in the form of an eight-pointed flower

Fig. 104   Bamboo Brush Pot Depicting Guo Ziyi Subduing the Enemy by Persuasion
Late Ming/early Qing dynasty
Bamboo
Height 15 cm, diameter 13.5 cm
Palace Museum, Taibei

The carving of this bamboo brush pot demonstrates the use of the compositional techniques of painting. Beneath some pine trees an elderly man on horseback, a staff in one hand and the reins in the other, faces a group of kneeling soldiers. This is a depiction of the famous Tang dynasty general Guo Ziyi (697–781) subduing his opponents through a combination of reputation and moral persuasion. The carving is powerful with a bold unrestrained sense of line.

Fig. 103   Red Sandalwood Brush Rest Inlaid with Jade
Qing dynasty
Wood and jade
Height 2.7 cm × Width 24.4 cm × Depth 5.5 cm
Palace Museum, Taibei

The feet of this brush tray are curved inwards. It will accommodate five brushes. The inlaid jade plaque carved with hornless dragons gives it a Han dynasty air. Although Wen Zhenheng regarded brush rest as old fashioned and obsolete and to be discarded, this illustration provides a glimpse of their appearance.

should not be used. The most valuable are ancient white pots from the Ding Kiln in the shape of a section of bamboo, though they are difficult to obtain. Holly-patterned porcelain pots and pots from the Xuande Kiln may be used as well. There are also drum-shaped pots with holes to hold brushes and ink sticks; they may be antique but they are inelegant.

Brush Boats or Trays

Brush boats of red sandalwood or ebony finely inlaid with strips of bamboo may be used but not those of ivory or jade.

Brush Washers

Brush washers in jade consist of: basin washers, oblong washers, and jade ring washers. Brush washers in ancient bronze consist of: small gilded washers, dark green basin washers, small cauldron-shaped washers, goblet washers and *yi*. None of these were originally designed as brush washers but used as such they are very elegant. Pottery

Fig. 105   Guan Kiln Brush Washer in the Form of a Sunflower

Southern Song dynasty
Overall Height 4.9 cm, diameter at mouth 12.1 cm, diameter at foot 3.7 cm
Palace Museum, Taibei

This brush washer is formed in the shape of a six-petal sunflower with a deep, curved wall and circular base with a shallow foot. It is thickly glazed, in and out, in a pale green celadon. The body is comparatively thin.

Fig. 106   Guan Kiln Circular Celadon Brush Washer

Southern Song dynasty
Height 9.2 cm, diameter at mouth 18.7 cm, diameter at base 10.9 cm
Palace Museum, Taibei

This circular washer has perpendicular sides and a flat base. It is glazed throughout in a rich pale green celadon glaze. Here and there one can see patches of lighter color and a densely distributed crackle pattern.

washers include: sunflower-patterned washers from the Guan and Ge kilns, Buddhist bell-mouthed washers, washers in the shape of lotus leaves, and rolled-lip split sugar cane washers (figs. 105, 106). Washers from the Longquan Kiln consist of: double fish washers, chrysanthemum washers, and pleated washers. Washers from the Ding Kiln consist of: three-hooped washers, plum blossom washers and washers in the shape of a square pool. The Xuande Kiln produced washers with a design of fish amongst reeds, sunflower leaf washers, Buddhist bell-mouthed washers and drum-shaped washers, all of which may be used. Washers bound in silk or with alternating bands of white and green are to be avoided. Some cups are used as brush washers or as brush palettes; they should not be used.

Brush Palettes

Palettes from the Ding and Longquan kilns in the form of small cups and dishes may be used. Those of crystal and colored glass are both inelegant and those made from leaves of jade are particularly vulgar.

Water Holders

Bronze water holders are all the rage but water becomes poisonous if kept in them for too long and then very easily makes brushes brittle. Consequently, porcelain holders are the best. Bronze buried for many years acquires the characteristics of porcelain; only

Fig. 107　Jade Water Holder in the Form of a Gourd
Ming dynasty
Overall height 4.9 cm × Length 8.6 cm × Depth 6.8 cm
Palace Museum, Taibei

The gleaming white jade of this oblate-shaped water holder is slightly tinged with patches of yellow. Its belly is carved with a pattern of gourds and lotus stems while the whole is covered in a pattern of vines and leaves. Its design is both simple and ordered.

the bronze of the Xuande reign may not be used. Holders made from jade include round-mouthed jars with a belly about the size of a fist. It is not known what use the ancients made of them though they are now used to hold water and are excellent (fig. 107). Small wine vessels (*zun*), cloud and thunder pattern wine jars (*lei*) and small cauldrons (*zeng*), all of bronze, may be used. There are also porcelain bowls and basins with large bellies and small mouths from the Guan and Ge kilns. The present-day jade basins made by Lu Zigang (dates unknown) of Suzhou in the form of ancient *lei* and *zun* and ornamented with the faces of beasts, although of fine workmanship, are of no account.

Water Jugs or Pourers[①]

There are ancient bronze and jade water pourers in the form of winged mythical lions (*bixie*), toads, crowing cocks, heavenly deer (a mythical

① Water pourer (*shuizhu*): used for pouring water on to an inkstone in order to grind ink. It has a spout or beak and this is what makes it different from a water holder.

animal not unlike a unicorn in appearance), cormorant shaped ladles and gilded jugs in the shape of geese. Those that can be held in the hand are excellent but sleeping oxen in bronze and those with a spout in the form of a boy riding an ox are utterly vulgar. Generally speaking, those made in human form are vessels of no elegance at all. There are rhinoceros, heavenly deer, turtles, dragons and heavenly horses with small bowls in their mouths, which were used by the ancients to fill lamps and are not water pourers. There are also porcelain pots from the Guan, Ge and Ding kilns in the shape of upright melons, melons on their sides, double peaches, lotus seed heads, plant stems, leaves and eggplants. The Xuande Kiln produces five-colored peach pourers and pourers in the shape of pomegranates, double gourds and twin mandarin ducks; none of these are as elegant as those of bronze.

Paste Boxes and Jars

Bronze vessels for holding paste include small portable lidded containers (*you*—an ancient wine vessel) the size of a fist with a handle in the form of twisted rope; jars with bellies resembling a small wine cup and a square base; buckets bound with three hoops and tripod feet; and finally, small square receptacles with a key pattern in the style of those fired by Jiang of the Yuan dynasty; all these may be used. Porcelain boxes include Ding Kiln bulb-topped jars and Ge Kiln square containers with a crossbar handle in the form of a *hu* (an ancient measuring vessel), but none of these will wash as well as those of bronze.

Wax Boxes

The ancients used wax as a substitute for paste. Consequently, letters were sealed with hot wax. Nowadays, though wax is no longer used, these boxes make good playthings and the larger ones may be used to hold water.

Paperweights

Paperweights of jade include rabbits, oxen, horses, deer, sheep, toads, crouching tigers, winged mythical lions, and hornless dragons large and small, all of great elegance and antiquity. Bronze paperweights include dark green frogs, crouching tigers and hornless dragons, sleeping dogs, gilded winged mythical lions, recumbent horses, turtles and dragons, all of which may be used (fig. 108). However, agate, crystal and those from the Guan, Ge and Ding kilns are not objects of any great elegance. Bronze weights of the Xuande reign in the form of horses, oxen, cats, dogs and *suanni* (a mythical animal, one of the nine sons of the dragon) are exceptionally fine.

Ruler Weights

Ruler weights are made from red sandalwood or ebony and may be ornamented with an old jade sword belt hook (*zhi*[1]) as a knob with a cord (fig. 109). These are vulgarly called *zhaowen* belts (belts of literary merit). There are ruler weights made in Japan with gilded knobs in the form of a double peach with silver leaves that, though of intricate workmanship, are objects of no elegance. There are others pierced with a hole containing a blade. These are extremely vulgar.

Wrist Rests

The long wrist rests of jade made in the form of an old sword belt hook are the finest; elsewhere the Japanese black lacquer rests in the form of a jade tablet (*gui*—an emblem

Fig. 108   Weight in the Form of an Auspicious Animal
Han dynasty
Height 4.5 cm, diameter at base 4.5 cm
Palace Museum, Taibei

Shaped like a hemisphere, this gilded bronze weight shows a recumbent tiger with spread forelegs and spirited eyes. In the Han dynasty, before tables and chairs became common, seating was on mats, the four corners of which were held down by weights to prevent them being caught by the wind. From the Song dynasty onwards scholars used these weights as paperweights.

indicating status and held by the ancient nobility at ceremonies in the presence of the emperor) are as light as paper and a marvel. Those of red sandalwood incised with flowers, or bamboo incised with flowers and plants and images of people are not to be used.

Fig. 109   Sword Belt Hook Decorated with a Pattern of Hornless Dragon
Han dynasty
Length 11.4 cm × Width 2.8 cm
Palace Museum, Taibei

This yellow jade sword belt hook is marked with patches of deep orange. Slender in shape, its two ends curve inwards. The surface is carved with a hornless dragon, thin-bodied with a fine tail, though the limbs are sturdy.

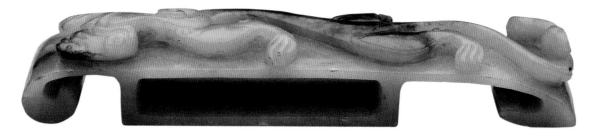

Paper Polishers

In ancient times, paper polishers were made of seashell but now crystal and agate are used. Some ancient jades may be used instead and are even more elegant.

Paper Knives

There are ancient knives-as-brushes, dark green throughout the body, pointed at the top and round at the bottom, just over one *chi* (about 30 cm) in length, which the ancients used to remove the green outer skin from bamboo when preparing bamboo strips for writing. Nowadays, they are only playthings and not for actual use. There is an extremely small kind, made in Japan, with a very sharp tip and a handle of chicken-wing wood (*Millettia laurentii*) that does not stain with grease, which is excellent. Paper knives of silver inlaid with gold from Dian (present-day Yunnan) may also be used. The knives from Liyang (in present-day Jiangsu) and Kunshan (on the border of present-day Jiangsu) are dreadful, whilst the knives of Lu Xiaozhuo[2] are even worse.

Scissors

There are ingeniously made scissors of fine iron with a gilded pattern of raised flowers on the outer surface while the inner surface is inlaid with a key pattern. The Japanese make a folding kind that is also useful.

Reading Lamps

There are ancient bronze reading lamps in the form of camels, sheep, and turtles as well as Zhuge lamps[3]. These are for amusement rather than use. There is a bronze lamp on a stand with a reflector in the shape of a lotus flower from which the ancients took the idea of lanterns, which are now used as reading lamps and are very elegant. The triple-cupped oil lamps from the Ding Kiln and the double-cupped lamps from the Xuande Kiln do not bear use. Ancient lanterns made from gleaming white flax and of simple shape and small size are of the best quality.

Lamps

The pearl lamps from the land of Min (present-day Fujian) are first in quality; those made from tortoiseshell, amber and fish skulls are less good. The parchment lamps painted by craftsmen such as Zhao Hu (dates unknown) are also worthy of collection. *Liaosi*[4] lamps from Dian are the best. Lamps produced in Danyang (in present-day Jiangsu Province) scatter light crosswise and are not an elegant sight. As to the Shandong manufactured lamps made from pearls, barley stalks, twisted thread and firewood, as well as those resembling plum and pear blossom, flowers and plants, birds and animals and lamps ornamented with paper cutouts as well as black-colored lanterns; none of these are of quality. Fine lamps are square like screens pierced with the shape of birds and flowers and refined as a painting. Images of people and buildings may only be used on parchment screens. The remainder, such as those resembling steamer baskets and water crystal balls and those in two or three layers are all dreadful. Lamps made from split bamboo may be intricate in construction but they have a poverty-stricken air. I once saw a lamp made from Yuan dynasty cloth that was unusual but unfashionable.

---

1 *Zhi* (璏) a form of jade hook bound to the scabbard of a sword by means of a keeper that allowed the sword to be attached to a belt. Later, with a cord through the keeper it made a convenient knob for lifting a ruler weight without the fingers touching the paper.

2 Lu Xiaozhuo, either the name of a Suzhou cutler or his shop, mentioned by the Ming commentator and playwright Zhang Dafu (c. 1554–c. 1630) in his *Jottings from the Plum Blossom Hut*.

3 Zhuge lamp, traditionally associated with the strategist Zhuge Liang (181–234) and thought to have been used for military purposes.

4 *Liaosi*, a material produced by boiling down agate into a paste from which fine translucent fibers are produced, spaghetti fashion, to cover lamps.

Mirrors

The best mirrors (fig. 110) are of ancient bronze, the color of black lacquer decorated with Qin dynasty designs but with a thick smooth plain back. Next in quality are bronze mirrors, which are decorated with a design

Fig. 111 Symbols of the True Aspect of the Five Sacred Mountains

The symbols of the five sacred mountains are not only to be found in books but also often appear in ornaments, ritual objects, library utensils, and stone rubbings. They have an enduring history of over two thousand years.

Fig. 110 Bronze Mirror with a Pattern of Stars and Clouds

Han dynasty
Diameter 17.8 cm
Palace Museum, Taibei

The ancients used bronzes polished to reflect an image as mirrors, the backs decorated in delicate patterns. The mirror was not only a utensil but an artistic object as well. In this example a decoration of linked small curves surrounds the knob of the handle. The mirror back is decorated with four panels of flowers intertwined with grass. The edge is decorated with a pattern of linked curves.

of flowers in silver on the back. There are small mirrors the size of a coin with bronze backs inlaid with a design of the five sacred mountains[1] (fig. 111) in gold and silver, which may be carried on the person. Mirrors with a water chestnut design, or octagonal in shape or square with a handle are vulgar and should not be used. Xuan Yuan[2] mirrors, like a globe in shape, may be hung in front of a bed to ward off evil spirits, but they are not of antique form.

Hooks

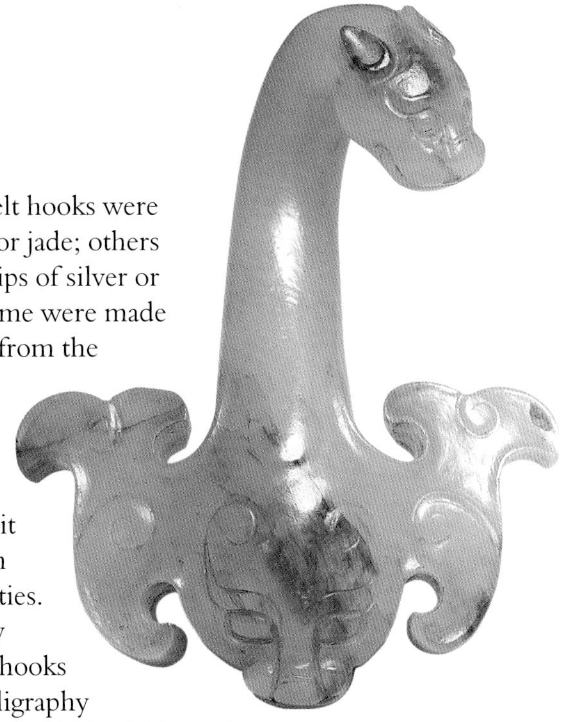

Some ancient bronze belt hooks were inlaid with gold, silver, or jade; others were decorated with strips of silver or gold (figs. 112, 113). Some were made in the shape of animals from the Xia, Shang and Zhou dynasties. Hooks inlaid with a design of a sheep's head or a praying mantis in pursuit of a cicada date are from the Qin and Han dynasties. They may be plentifully displayed in a studio as hooks from which to hang calligraphy and paintings or as (handles for) whisks and fans. As such, they are most elegant. They measure from one *cun* (about 3 cm) to one *chi* (about 30 cm) in length and may all be used.

Belts and Sashes

Han dynasty hooks and slit rings (*jue*) that only measure just over two *cun* (about 6 cm) make convenient belt or sash fasteners. The slightly larger ones have become curios and are not for daily use. Sashes should be either the color of agarwood or a deep purple. Other colors are unsuitable.

Fig. 112   Jade Belt Hook
Warring States period to early Western Han dynasty
Height 2.5 cm × Length 4.1 cm × Depth 3.3 cm
Palace Museum, Taibei

Belt hooks were used by the ancient nobility and literati to secure waist sashes. Although they were mainly made of bronze, other materials such as gold, silver, iron, and jade were also used. Belt hooks originated in the Western Zhou dynasty. They were a status symbol as much as a requisite of daily life.

---

1 Mount Tai in Shandong, Mount Hua in Shaanxi, Mount Heng in Hunan, Mount Heng in Shanxi and Mount Song in Henan.
2 Xuan Yuan, a name associated with the mythical Yellow Emperor.

Fig. 113   Gilt Belt Hook
Han dynasty
Height 25 cm
Palace Museum, Taibei

A small animal forms the head of this belt hook. An animal face can be seen on the front and rear of the tongue on the back of the hook, together with a representation of the curling fur on its body. The body of the hook is gilded.

Zen Lamps

The finest Zen lamps come from the land of Goryeo; there are moon lamps, that shine as white as the new moon; there are lamps like the sun, that once lit color the room red, the small ones are particularly attractive. There is a bronze tripod burner from Goryeo with drooping lotus leaves that served as a stand. It is now unobtainable and others must be sought as a stand and not made like many-cornered lamps.

Citron Dishes

There are ancient bronze citron dishes as well as citron dishes of *qingdong* porcelain from the Guan, Ge and Ding kilns (fig. 114). There are also large celadon dishes from the Longquan Kiln and dishes decorated with a hidden underglaze pattern from the Xuande reign as well as blue-and-white porcelain and vermilion dishes. All of these may be used. When citrons ripens no hill studio should ever be without some. Placing four citrons in a single dish is dull and conventional and putting twenty or thirty in a large dish is vulgar in the extreme. It is better to find an old red tea dish on which to place a single citron to appreciate, or an old long porcelain dish that takes two and then put it on a table.

Ruyi Scepters

These scepters were used by the ancients to indicate direction or to guard against the unexpected and were thus forged from iron; they were not merely to admire. I once found a fine old one with a gold and silver inlay that was hidden one moment and visible the next; it was elegant in its simplicity. Those made from tree branches or lengths of bamboo are rubbish.

Fig. 114 Dish with a Pattern of a One-Legged Dragon (*Kui*)
Spring and Autumn period (770–476 BC)
Height 11.1 cm
Palace Museum, Taibei
This bronze dish has vertical lugs, or ears, and curved sides decorated with a pattern of one-legged dragons. It has an air of great antiquity.

Fig. 115 Knife Currency of the State of Yan

Warring States period

Knife currency was one of the cast bronze currencies of the Spring and Autumn and Warring States periods and was cast in the form of a small knife. Generally speaking it is composed of the head, body, handle, and ring.

Whisks

Whisks were used by the ancients as an aid to conversation. Nowadays, flourished at a guest they are enough to make you vomit. However, they may be hung on the wall of a studio as part of a collection. There are old ones with handles of jade and tails of black or white hair that are quite elegant. Those made from bamboo or cane may be of exquisite workmanship but they should not be used.

Coins

Coins come in many shapes and sizes, the *Compendium of Coins*[1] may be consulted for details. There is a kind of bronze currency in the shape of a knife (fig. 115) and inlaid with gold that may be used as a bookmark and can be used (to mark a place) in a book of many volumes such as the *Ancient Objects Illustrated*[2]. Small coins and ancient pre-Qin coinage in the form of a shovel may be hung from the top of a staff.

Ladles and Dippers

Ladles and dippers may be made out of small flat gourds, large ones no more than four or five *cun* (about 15 cm) in length and the small ones half that size. The inside may be washed out with water and the outside polished with a cloth. It will gleam with cleanliness, water will not affect it and dirt will not stain it and it may be hung from a staff or from a Zen chair made from tree roots. There is also an elegant double dipper that may be worn on the head to secure the hair. The long-waisted ones with a twisted neck like a heron or cormorant should not be used.

Bowls for Buddhist Monks

Bowls for Buddhist monks, made from the roots of giant bamboo found in the deep mountains and turned on a lathe, if inscribed with characters or Sanskrit texts or images of the Five Sacred Mountains all infilled with azurite, are very attractive.

---

1 A number of books were published under this name over the centuries.
2 Probably the Song dynasty work in 30 volumes illustrating objects in the imperial collection prepared at the direction of the Song Emperor Huizong.

Flower Vases

When bronze flower vases have been buried for a number of years and are then used for flowers, the flowers themselves become fresh and bright; it is not just the antiquity of the bronze that is so appealing. Bronze vessels in which flowers may be placed consist of: *zun* (wine vessels), *lei* (wine jars), *gu* (goblets) and *hu* (pots or jugs), which may be selected on the basis of the size of the bunch of flowers. Porcelain vases mostly include antique bladder-shaped vases from the Guan, Ge and Ding kilns, single stem vases and small yarrow vases (square bodied, short-necked vases with a round foot, or vases in th shape of a squared tube) (fig. 116) as well as paper mallet-shaped vases (fig. 117). The remainder, for example vases with hidden underglaze decoration, blue-and-white vases, pouch-shaped vases, gourd vases, narrow-mouthed vases, flat-bellied vases, thin-legged vases, medicine jars, newly cast bronze vases and flower vases from the Jian Kiln are not suitable for elegant display. Goose-necked wall vases are to be used even less. Han dynasty square bronze vases, and vases from the Longquan and Jun kilns, two or three *chi* (about 90 cm) at

Fig. 116 Celadon Vase in the Shape of a Squared Tube (*Cong*)
Southern Song dynasty
Guan Kiln
Overall height 18.8 cm, diameter at mouth 12.8 cm, diameter at base 12.4 cm
Palace Museum, Taibei

A *cong* is a squared tube in jade and was an important ritual object in ancient China. This flower vase imitates the shape of a five-sectioned *cong* with a square body but round mouth. It is thickly glazed in pale green and is covered in a dense crackle pattern.

Fig. 117 Celadon Vase in the Shape of a Paper Mallet
Northern Song dynasty
Ru Kiln
Height 20.4 cm, diameter at mouth 4 cm, diameter at base 8.7 cm, width at shoulder 13.0 cm
Palace Museum, Taibei

The vase derives its name from the mallet used to beat fiber pulp in the process of making paper. The body of the vase is glazed in a pale green of lustrous simplicity. The surface of the glaze is covered with a light, transparent crackle pattern.

the most in height, are well suited to hold plum blossom. Using an internal tin water container within the vase avoids the danger of splits in the wall of the vase. For the best, flower vases should be slender rather than squat, large rather than small and up to one *chi* five *cun* (about 45 cm) but not less than one *chi* (about 30 cm) in height.

Bells and Chimes

Bells and chimes[1] may not be set up opposite each other. One should collect bronze bells cast in the Qin and Han dynasties as well as *bianzhong* (bells with an oval rather than circular mouth) and chimes of Lingbi stone for clarity of sound and carrying power; hung in a studio or room they please the ear when struck (fig. 118). There are antique chimes of jade where the *gu* (the short broad portion of the chime's carpenters' set square shape) measures three *cun* (about 9 cm) with a length of over one *chi* (about 30 cm); these are for display only.

Walking Sticks

"Turtle dove" walking sticks (with handles ornamented with a turtle dove pattern) are the most ancient, so called because old people often choke and turtle doves are able to cure choking. There are stick handles from the Xia, Shang and Zhou dynasties decorated with upright and flying doves inlaid with gold and silver that, mounted on square bamboo (*Chimonobambusa quadrangularis*), *qiong* bamboo (*Qiongzhuea tumidinoda*) or rattan, are extremely elegant. A fine walking stick should be over seven *chi* (about 2.1 m) in length and highly polished. There is a kind of naturally twisted rattan from Mount Tiantai that can be made into all kinds of dragons' heads; this cannot be used at all.

Stools

In winter, stools are made from rushes and have a height of one *chi* two *cun* (about 36 cm), the four sides are tightly woven and the wooden seat is supported by internal pillars, the outer surface is covered in brocade. Rattan stools may be used during the hot months. In palaces there are elaborately elegant embroidered stools, in appearance like a small drum with tassels at the corners; these may also be used.

---

1 Chinese chimes usually comprise a tuned set mounted on a frame and sounded by a mallet.

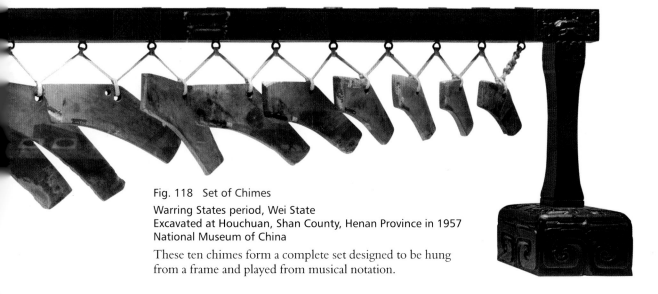

Fig. 118 Set of Chimes
Warring States period, Wei State
Excavated at Houchuan, Shan County, Henan Province in 1957
National Museum of China

These ten chimes form a complete set designed to be hung from a frame and played from musical notation.

Fig. 119 Jin'gangzi Prayer Beads
Palace Museum, Taibei

According to Buddhist scriptures, *jingangzi* are the seeds of the *jingang* tree (*Elaeocarpus ganitrus*) though they are also said to be the seeds of the Bodhi tree. They are extremely rare. *Jingang* can also mean adamantine or invincible. Thus, wearing *jingang* beads whose strength in warding off evil and preventing disaster was regarded as comparatively strong was thought to increase good fortune.

Sitting Pads

There are rush sitting pads of a diameter of three *chi* (about 90 cm) that are convenient for sitting on the floor. Those made of coir are excellent. For the avoidance of insects and damp in the hills a waxed cloth pad may be made with a wax of red orpiment, which is very elegant.

Prayer Beads

Prayer beads made of the finely patterned seeds of the Bodhi tree (*Ficus religiosa*) are the most valuable (fig. 119). There are also Song dynasty Buddhist phurpas (a talisman for subduing demons) of jade, and jade reckoning beads representing the five items used in Buddhist worship. These are: anointing incense, flowers, burning incense, offerings of food, and lamplight. Others such as beads made from skulls, pearls, agate, amber, yellow amber, crystal, coral and clamshells are all vulgar. However, agarwood may be used. Beads made from the seeds of the Hangzhou Bodhi tree and beads that have been soaked in perfume are to be avoided the most.

Foreign Scriptures

Foreign monks are often to be seen with scriptures at their belt, or in a leather bag or in a lacquer box about three *cun* (about 9 cm) square and just over one *cun* (about 3 cm) in thickness. The box has lugs on each side to take a cord. They also carry Buddhist sutras inscribed on palm leaves in gold characters, as well as paintings in color and depictions of demons in disguise, all skillfully executed and unmatched

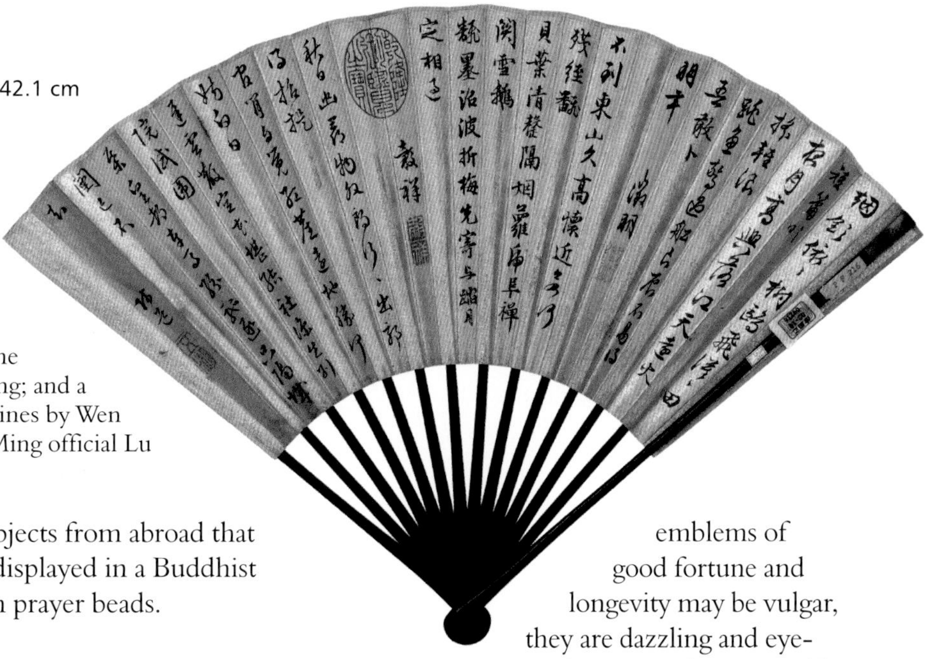

Fig. 120 Fan

Paper
Height 16.5 cm × Width 42.1 cm
Palace Museum, Taibei

The fan bears verses
in the calligraphy of
three members of
the literati; verses
in five character
lines by Wen
Zhengming, grandfather
of Wen Zhenheng, and the
calligrapher Wang Guxiang; and a
verse in seven character lines by Wen
Zhengming's pupil the Ming official Lu
Shidao.

in China. These are objects from abroad that may be collected and displayed in a Buddhist chamber together with prayer beads.

Fans and Fan Pendants

Feather fans are the most elegant but ancient folding fans with carved lacquer handles are also of quality. Other fans, such as those of bamboo strips, glued paper, and those with handles of bamboo root or sandalwood are all vulgar. There are also the folding fans nowadays imported from Japan that the ancients used to call "mass headed fans." There are also other fine fans from that country that measure a full *chi* (about 30 cm) across when open but a mere two fingers in width and a bit when closed. They are mostly painted with court ladies, carriages, prancing horses, and scenes of walking in the woods and spring picnics. Other fans depict the legend of the cowherd and the weaver girl (illfated lovers represented by the stars Vega and Altair separated by the Milky Way) painted over a ground of gold and silver in a generally good resemblance, the sky blue and sea green being of rare beauty and mixed from malachite and glauconite. The tribute items prepared by the prefectures of the region of Shu in Sichuan include fans with handles attached by golden rivets to a leaf as light as silk; these are most valuable. Although the Palace Manufactory fans painted in color with designs of the five poisonous creatures (centipedes, snakes, scorpions, lizards and toads), the hundred cranes and deer and

emblems of good fortune and longevity may be vulgar, they are dazzling and eye-catching. Huizhou (now She County in Anhui Province) and Hangzhou produce delicate light fans, such as those from Mount Gusu (in present-day Suzhou) where fans incorporating calligraphy (fig. 120) and painting are regarded as important. The handles (spines) are made from white bamboo (*Rhyllostachys nudilaria*), palm wood (*Rhapis humilis*), ebony, sandalwood, sapphire-berry (*Symplocos paniculata*), speckled bamboo and other woods as well as ivory and tortoiseshell. There are also round-headed, square, corded and knotted handles and fans where each rib bears incised decorations. One should seek out and buy fans with a plain white or gold leaf, painted or inscribed by the famous. The best fetch a high price. Makers include Li Zhao, Li Zan, Ma Xun, Jiang San, Liu Yutai and Shen Shaolou, all of them highly skilled craftsmen. If the paper is worn and ink muddy and will not bear handling, the leaf should be placed in a book to be enjoyed. This has been the fashionable practice in Suzhou for some time, in fact it is rather vulgar and it would be better to use fans from Sichuan.

Fan pendants are best made from fragrant agarwood although Han dynasty split rings of jade or pieces of amber may also be used. Incense beads and beads made from the afzelia tree (*Pahudia xylocarpa*) may on no account be used.

Pillows

There are so-called "writing pillows" consisting of three rolls of paper resembling a bowl in shape and tied together like the character *pin* (品 —three scrolls seen end-on). There are also "old kiln pillows" measuring two *chi* five *cun* (about 75 cm) in length and six *cun* (about 18 cm) across, which may also be used. There is a pillow one *chi* (about 30 cm) in length, called a "corpse pillow." This is an ancient burial item and is not to be used.

Bamboo Mats

Zizania (wild rice straw) comes from the sultanate of Malacca where it grows by the waterside. The leaves are soft and may be woven into fine mats for winter use when they will feel warm and comfortable. In the summer, mats of Qizhou bamboo are the best.

Qin

The *qin*[①] is an ancient musical instrument and even if not played it may be hung on a wall (fig. 121). The *qin* has a long history and the most valuable are those that, though the lacquer is faded, are as black as plum blossom-patterned ebony and have a light tone to the strings. Pegs of rhinoceros horn and ivory are good. The inlaid studs may be of pearl rather than gold or silver. Strings should be made from the white silk of silkworms fed on mulberry leaves (*Cudrania tricuspidata*). Although the ancients spoke of the melodious quality of treated strings they are not as good as the natural wonder of plain strings. Renowned makers of the *qin* include Lei Wen and Zhang Yue of the Tang dynasty; Shi Muzhou of the Song dynasty; Zhu Zhiyuan of the Yuan dynasty; and from the present dynasty, Hui Xiang, Gao Teng, Zhu Haihe and Fan and Lu. When hanging the instruments they should be placed away from sunlight and draughts. *Qin* bags should be made from ancient brocade. Red and green tassels should not be used on the pegs. The instrument should not be carried cross-wise and in the summer it is better to play early in the morning or late in the evening. Playing at midday risks the dirt from sweat, and strings may snap because of the dry heat.

① *Qin*, an ancient musical instrument, formerly five-stringed, latterly seven-stringed.

Fig. 121 Ancient *Qin*

Ming dynasty
Length 121.2 cm × Width 18.2 cm × Height 6.4 cm
Metropolitan Museum of Art, New York

The *qin* is the earliest Chinese plucked string instrument with a history of over 3,000 years. It has a unique and characteristic sound, a broad compass, and a deep timbre. When listening to it one enters a world of remote tranquility.

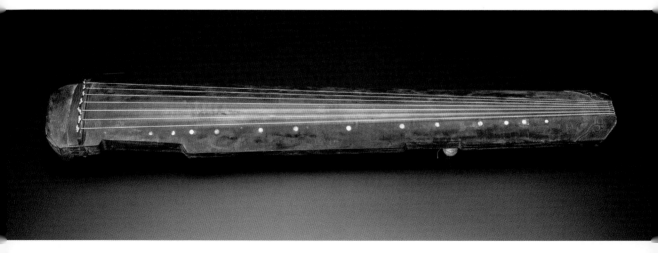

Qin Tables and Stands

The bricks fired by Guo Gong of Zhengzhou in Henan, their surface decorated with a pattern of overlapping lozenges and elephants' eyes, are wonderful and may be made into a stand for a *qin*, the hollow space within acting as a resonator. The stand may also serve to display ancient stones and *penjing*. For elegance there should also be a small table measuring one *chi* (about 30 cm) longer than the *qin* itself and with a height of two *chi* eight *cun* (about 84 cm) and wide enough to accommodate three *qin*s. A folding chair may be used as a seat since it is slightly higher than other seats and allows ease of movement and does not tire the hands. There are tabletops of crystal bordered with sandalwood and inset with pools of silver filled with water in which fish are kept and plants grow. They are truly vulgar constructions.

Inkstones

Inkstones (fig. 122) made of Duanxi stone from Zhaoqing prefecture in Guangdong are the best (present-day Gaoyao County of Guangdong Province). There are old and new quarries and there is a difference between the upper and lower cliffs. The most valuable stone is deep purple in color, smooth to the touch and rings brightly when struck, with a blue-green parrot's eye pattern surrounded by a halo. Next in quality are red stones that when in contact with warm breath exhibit a water stain; coarsely patterned examples are known as "west quarry stone" and are not particularly valuable. There are also natural rocks, as smooth as jade, which emit no sound when polished and grind ink that does not damage the brush; these are rare treasures. There are some good inkstones without the eye patterning, as for example those of white Duanxi stone or blue-green Duanxi stone; consequently, the presence of eye patterning does not determine quality. So-called black

Fig. 122 Inkstone with Inscription Attributed to Su Shi
Song dynasty
Height 2.7 cm × Length 11.3 cm × Width at its broadest 7.8 cm
Palace Museum, Taibei

This inkstone is oval in shape and a deep purple ochre in color. The slightly raised portion of the stone drains into the deep ink pool with the two characters *dong jing* (east well) incised above. The surround is decorated with a pattern of clouds and stars. The whole abounds with a sense of antiquity. There are two feet beneath.

Duanxi stone comes from Chenzhou and Yuanzhou in Huguang (present-day Hunan and Hubei) and also has eye patterning but the stone is coarse and dry and is not real Duanxi stone. Another kind of stone comes from the Sheshan hills and Longweixi in Wuyuan (now in Shangrao City, Jiangxi Province). Here too, there are old and new quarries that were opened in the Southern Tang dynasty and were exhausted by the time of the Northern Song dynasty, hence old inkstones are not from the Song dynasty but from these quarries. The most valuable inkstones of those speckled with silver and gold, with ribbed patterning or a patterning of fine lines or like eyebrows, are green-black in color. Lixi stone comes from Chenzhou and Changde (now in Hunan Province) in Huguang. The stone is light green in color but deep purple within. Those threaded with gold and veined in yellow are commonly called "purple robe and golden sash." Taoxi inkstones come from the rivers of Lintao prefecture in Shaanxi and are green and as smooth as jade. Qu inkstones come from Kaihua County in Quzhou (now in Zhejiang Province); there are some extremely large ones, black in color. Inkstones of wrought iron come from Qingzhou (present-day Weifang City of Shandong Province) and those made from ancient tiles come from Xiangzhou (present-day Anyang City of Henan Province). Chengni inkstones come from Guozhou (Luoyang City of Henan Province).

There are different forms and different methods of manufacture for inkstones. During the Song dynasty inkstones manufactured for the imperial palace took the form of jade terraces, phoenix pools, jade rings and jade buildings; these are the highly regarded "tribute inkstones" of today. There is a valuable kind of inkstone, seven *cun* (about 21 cm) high and four *cun* (about 12 cm) broad with the capacity of the size of a fist. I do not know whether it was specially ordered as tribute but its manufacture is exceptionally vulgar. The other inkstones of the Xuanhe period that I have seen have included the both extremely large and extremely small ones in the shape of an eight-pointed star, all elegantly simple in appearance. Others took the form of round pools or the gourd used by Su Shi, or axes or the shape of the Duanming palace; all may be used. Gourd-shaped inkstones are rather vulgar and it is an abominable practice to carve inkstones with the Twenty-Eight Stellar Mansions[①] or birds, beasts, turtles, dragons and celestial horses or to scrape

[①] Twenty-Eight Stellar Mansions, an ancient astronomical ordering of the heavens with seven Mansions to each of the Four Directions.

away a portion of the inkstone surface and insert a bronze or jade inlay in the form of the Seven Stars (Big Dipper). Inkstones should be rinsed daily to rid them of the dregs of accumulated ink so that they gleam blackly. However, the ineradicable speckled ink stains at the side of the ink pool are known as *moxiu* (ink embroidery) and should not be ground away. Inkstones should be filled with water for use and dried after use. Cleaning an inkstone with a lotus seedpod will revive it and rid it of dirt without damaging it. The use of boiling water or tea or wine for grinding ink is to be avoided, nor should an urchin be instructed to wash it by hand. Inkstone boxes may be made of purple or black lacquer but not metal as it dries out the stone, nor should sandalwood, ebony, or carved red or colored lacquer be used; all are vulgar.

Writing Brushes

The four virtues of the writing brush consist of "pointedness," "evenness," "roundedness," and "strength," by reason of the fact that when the hairs are firm the brush is pointed, when the hairs are numerous the brush is even; when hemp is properly used to stiffen the inside, the brush is round and when perfect hairs are properly attached with fragrant civet musk and glue the brush will become strong with long use. These are the secrets of brush making. In the ancient past there were brush handles (tubes) of gold and silver, ivory, tortoiseshell, and glass, as well as lacquered gold thread and deep green handles. Nowadays, there are handles of sandalwood and ornamented handles; these are vulgar and not to be used. In truth, speckled bamboo handles are the finest though *Indocalamus latifolia* may also be used. For large brushes between eight *chi* and one *zhang* the use of wood is vulgar. They should be made from *qiong* bamboo since the bamboo is slender and the segments between joints are large and make for easy handling. The tip of the brush should resemble a pointed bamboo shoot; the narrow-waisted gourd-shaped kind is only good for writing small, though it is in common use at present. Hangzhou produces the best brushes for painting. The ancients used a brush washer because of the need to rinse the brush to rid it of clogged ink after writing so that the hairs remained strong and long-lasting and were not shed. Once a brush is exhausted it should be buried. The saying: "an exhausted brush is for the grave" is not empty speech.

Ink Sticks

Good ink sticks are light in texture and clear in color. The sticks should be without odor and make no sound when ground (fig. 123). For example, take painting and calligraphy from the Jin, Tang, Song and Yuan dynasties, which has been handed down for hundreds of years and remains undimmed in vigor, its ink still as black as lacquer; this is the consequence of good ink. Hence, one must choose fine ink sticks and since they are often displayed on tables they should have a certain elegance of shape as well. Consequently, there are makes of ink stick, such as Court Official (*chaoguan*), Big Dipper (*kuixing*), Precious Vase (*baoping*) and Jade Ring Ink (*mojue*), which may not be used despite their excellent color. Xuande ink is the finest and almost the same as that from the Palace Manufactory of the Xuanhe period. It is now a collector's item though it may be used for copying ancient paintings and calligraphy, its strength having utterly faded leaving just the luster of the ink and nothing else. In the Tang dynasty the ink of Xi Tinggui was the best followed by that of Zhang Yu. The imperial name of Li was bestowed on Xi Tinggui and his ink is now as valuable as treasure itself.

Paper

The ancients cut bamboo, scraped away the green outer surface and then cured and dried

Fig. 123 Ink as a National Treasure Item
Ming dynasty, Yongle period
Length 18.2 cm
Palace Museum, Taibei

Ink stick shaped like a long, thick ox-tongue with rounded corners. One side has a molded imprint of two bicorn dragons with long whiskers and densely set scales. The tips of their claws are incomparably sharp and a pattern of flames surrounds the dragon's body.

it and split it into slips upon which to write. Later they used paper. Paper in the north is made with the strips of the mesh screen (paper mold) running from side to side so that the patterning runs cross-wise. The paper is pliable and thick and is called "side-patterned." In southern paper the strips run from top to bottom. Genuine calligraphy of the two Wangs (Wang Xizhi and Wang Xianzhi) is mostly of this kind. The Tang dynasty produced a hard yellow paper with dye from the cork tree (*Phellodendron amurense*), which was insect proof. Xue Tao (c. 768–832) the Tang dynasty poetess from the land of Shu (Sichuan) made paper called "ten colored writing paper" (small and expensive sheets produced in single colors such as white, yellow or pink as well as patterned sheets). In the Song dynasty there was paper known as Paper of the Hall of Clarity of Heart as well as yellow and white paper for the classics that needs to be unfolded before use. There was also patterned writing paper called Azure Clouds and Spring Trees, Dragon and Phoenix, Flower Roundel and Golden Flower. There were also larger sizes of paper measuring from three to five *zhang* (about 6–15 m) in length. There was writing paper colored in pink and there is also paper known as rattan white, swan white and silkworm (white). In the Yuan dynasty the prefecture of Shaoxing (in present-day Zhejiang) produced pink colored writing paper, wax writing paper, yellow writing paper, flowered writing paper and ribbed writing paper, while White Talisman, Guanyin and Qing River paper was produced in Jiangxi. This kind of paper should be stored in a mountain retreat for use. In this Ming dynasty, paper made for official purposes in Jiangxi and Fujian (*lianqizhi*), Guanyin paper, court memorandum paper (*zouben zhi*) and proclamation paper (*bangzhi*) are of no quality, though the pink writing paper finely sprinkled with gold dust used in the imperial palace, as stiff as a board and smoothed to the perfection of white jade, as well as other colored writing paper sprinkled with gold and the deep blue dyed paper as smooth as satin known as *ciqingzhi* are all to be treasured. Neither today's gold sprinkled paper from Suzhou nor the double thickness Tan paper made in Songjiang is particularly hard-wearing, the best is the *liansi* paper from

Jing County (present-day Xuancheng City in Anhui). There is a kind of paper made in Goryeo from the cocoons of silkworms, which has the pure white of damask and the durability of silk. When written upon the ink shines forth. This is a rare product that China does not possess.

Double-Edged Short Swords

These days there are no swordsmen and hence few famous swords, even the method of forging swords is no longer handed down from generation to generation. Ancient swords were made from a mixture of iron and bronze and Tao Hongjing (456–536) notes in the *Record of Swords and Sabers* "they are as curved as a hook, as straight as a bowstring and clangorous." None of this have I seen. Nowadays, there is nothing that surpasses the swords forged by the Japanese; their dark brightness can transfix you. I once saw an ancient bronze sword enveloped in verdigris that was worthy of collection.

Seals

Elegant seals are made from Qingtian stone (Qingtian County in Zhejiang), which gleams like jade and shines with the brightness of lamplight, though the ancients did not value it. Seals may be made of metal, ivory, jade, crystal, wood and stone (fig. 124). However, porcelain seals are easily broken and should not be used, thus none of the seals produced by the Guan, Ge, and Qingdong kilns are of any quality. Ancient seals made from cast gold, gold plate, gold and silver inlay, Shang gold (an ancient form of inlay), malachite, gold and jade and agate with elegantly carved characters and exquisite handles are all worthy of collection and appreciation.

The square seal inkpots from the Guan and Ge kilns are valuable, but the round pots or those with inset edges from the Ding Kiln are not so good. Oblong pots, pots with lids

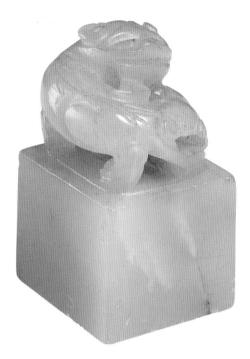

Fig. 124 Seal of Blue-Green Jade
Qing dynasty
Overall height 2.9 cm × Width 1.9 cm
Palace Museum, Taibei

This square seal of blue-green jade is decorated with a life-like representation of an animal head. Seals are a part of a visual art unique to China. They are not only a mark of individual status but also an object that combines in itself the arts of carving and calligraphy.

and pots with a blue-and-white pattern are all vulgar. Although the workmanship of recent jade inkpots with an overall pattern of a writhing hornless dragon is incomparable, they are of no quality. There are square jade pots from the Xia, Shang and Zhou dynasties that I have seen that are soil-stained blood red inside and out, which, though I do not know their purpose, make fine seal inkpots. However, they are part of the equipment of the scholar rather than something for daily use. Square library boxes with lids may be made of *Phoebe zhennan*, mahogany, and the wood of the tree fern (*Cyathea spinulosa*); if not, polished plain faded lacquer may be used. Other materials such as carved or filled lacquer, red sandalwood inlaid with ancient jade, moso bamboo and *jian* bamboo (*Phyllostachys heteroclada f. solida*) have neither elegance nor taste.

Stationery Boxes

Stationery boxes are fashionable but there are still really fine examples from the hands of ancient craftsmen available, made from *Phoebe zhennan*, burl wood, mahogany and tree fern. The others such as red sandalwood and rosewood are vulgar. The boxes contain three levels each with a drawer, which may contain a small Duanxi inkstone, a brush dish for mixing ink, a notebook, an inkstone in the form of a hill, a stick of Xuande ink and a small Japanese lacquer ink box. The top level contains a jade wrist rest, a jade or bronze paperweight, wrought iron knives, one small one large, a jade-handled brush, a brush boat and two Goryeo-made brushes. The next level contains an ancient bronze water dish, a paste spoon and a wax spoon, an ancient bronze water dipper and an ancient gilded green bronze brush washer. The lowest level should be slightly deeper and should contain a small Xuande period bronze burner, a Song dynasty carved red lacquer box, a small Japanese lacquer carrying box, a small white or colored porcelain box from the Ding Kiln, a small decorated Japanese wine cup and goblet and a library box, itself containing some fine examples of ancient jade seal inkpots and seals and gold inlaid seals, as well as a small Japanese comb box containing small tortoiseshell combs and ancient jade basins as well as two small rhinoceros or jade cups. Other fine antiques may also be included for the pleasure they give.

Combs and Accessories

Combs are made from burl wood or are made in Japan, however, red and white agate, bamboo strips, inlaid mother-of-pearl, carved lacquer and red sandalwood may not be used. Combs ornamented with tortoiseshell, jade comb cleaners, and jade pots and boxes, even if they are not from the Qin or Han dynasties, are acceptable provided they have some antiquity.

The mistaken inclusion of the vulgarly new would not suit the uses of a man of taste.

Summary of Bronze, Jade, Carved and Engraved and Kiln Objects

The manufacture of jade objects both during the Qin and Han and the three first dynasties (Xia, Shang and Zhou) was by no means ordinary in its elegant excellence. For example, patterning in the form of a mother hornless dragon and child or a reclining silkworm, or the technique of milling the double hook motif with its sinuous flowing curves as fine as a hair have all been well known in society for some time. Jades stained blood red through burial in soil are the most numerous; I have seen only one or two examples of kingfisher or watered silver-colored or bronze-stained jades. Coxcomb red jade is the best, followed by the yellow of steamed chestnut and the white of sliced fat. The black of a dot of lacquer, the blue-green of fresh willow and the green of velvet are the next best. The presently esteemed green stone, as translucent as crystal, which the ancients called *bi*[1] (碧) is not jade at all. The most valuable jade objects are tablets (*gui*) and disks (*bi*), then tripod cauldrons (*ding*) and wine vessels (*yi*), goblets (*gu*) and wine vessels (*zun*), jugs (*beizhu*), and rings (*huan*) and slit rings (*jue*). Next are belt hooks, paperweights, sword belt hooks, *chonger* (the jade ornaments suspended at ear level from either side of a flat-topped crown or cap), jade talismans (*gangmao*—small inscribed square jade tablets attached to the clothing by a thread and intended to ward off sickness and evil), jade ear pendants, jade scabbard ornaments and jade seals and finally jade picks (a tool for undoing the knots on a *qin* or sword) and fan pendants.

The most valuable objects in bronze are tripod cauldrons (*ding*), wine vessels (*yi*), goblets (*gu*) and wine vessels (*zun*) as well as *dun* (vessels for holding grain) and *ge* (cooking pots for meat). Next come ewers (*yi*), lidded wine jars (*you*), large wine jars (*lei*) and goblets (*zhi*). Less valuable still are the ceremonial containers for grain called *fu* and *gui*, wine cup pourers (*zhongzhu*), the bowls that hold the blood used in the ancient ceremonies for oaths of allegiance or alliance, and perfume holders (*lianhuanang*). The difference between the three dynasties lies in the undecorated simplicity of the Shang dynasty, the fine carving and incisions of the Zhou dynasty and the delicate hair-like gold and silver inlay of the Xia dynasty. Short inscriptions are of one to two characters whilst long inscriptions can amount to twenty to thirty. Inscriptions of two to three hundred characters definitely indicate pieces from the late Zhou up to the beginning of the Qin dynasty.

In seal script the Xia dynasty used the bird foot form, the Shang dynasty insects and fish and the Zhou dynasty used the large seal script. The Qin dynasty used both large and small seal scripts but the Han dynasty used the small seal script. The first three dynasties used intaglio (incision) whereas the Qin and Han dynasties used relief though there was some intaglio. In some cases, inscriptions on stone tablets (stele) were incised with a blade, though there are objects that lack an inscription in which case they are folk ware of no particularly remarkable achievement and it is impossible to say immediately whether they possess antiquity or not. There are those who say that bronze ware buried for a long time is affected by the earth's moist energy and turns blue-green and that bronze immersed in water for a long time is corroded by its wetness and turns green. In no way is it thus, it is simply that the nature of bronze is a gleaming purity that easily turns blue-green or green; that is all.

In the colors of bronze, brown is less than cinnabar and cinnabar less than green and green less than blue-green. Blue-green is less than the color of quicksilver and quicksilver less than lacquer black but lacquer black is the easiest to counterfeit. It is my view that blue-green and green should be the most highly rated. Counterfeiting employs the cold welding of additions with lead (*lengchong*)①, the reassembly of fragments (*xiecou*)② and the firing (of bronze) to produce speckles (*shaoban*); all these methods are easy to detect.

The pottery from the Chai Kiln③ is the most valuable and though I have never seen an example I have heard of its qualities; a heavenly blue-green, the brightness of a mirror, the thinness of paper and the chime of a bell; can it be thus? I do not know. The best of the ware from the Guan, Ge and Ru kilns is the powder blue, then the weak white, while the oil gray (*youhui*) is the least. In patterning, ice crackle, eel's blood red (*shanxue*) and unglazed brown (*tiezu*) are the best, then plum blossom pattern and ink black followed by the variegated crackle pattern. The Guan Kiln's hidden pattern of crab's claws, the Ge Kiln's hidden fish pattern and the white teardrop glaze of the Ding Kiln are all good but the purple and black are of no value. The rouge of the Junzhou Kiln is best, followed by scallion green and purple-black. The variegated colors are not valuable. Longquan ware is thick and not easily damaged but because of a certain lack

① *Lengchong*: the practice of using lead to attach missing pieces to damaged early bronzes, wax to add decoration and embellish color as well as rubbing them with a substance known as Shanhuang mud (*shanhuangni*) in order to reproduce a freshly excavated appearance.

② *Xiecou*: seeking out fragments of ancient bronzes such as the "ears," feet, handles and belly from old tombs; using the covers of ancient pots to form a round tripod vessel (*ding*); using old bronze mirrors to form the square pieces required to build a square tripod vessel as well as using the other techniques described above in *lengchong*.

③ *Chai Kiln*: said to have operated in the Later Zhou dynasty of the Five dynasties during the reign of Shizong (921–959). The porcelain nowadays described as "the color of the sky after rain" is copied after Chai ware. There is also the saying "the maker of vessels is named Chai and so it is called the Chai Kiln"—now in Zhengzhou of Henan Province.

of skill on the part of the craftsmen it is not particularly elegant. The ice crackle and eel's blood of the Xuande Kiln are much the same as those of the Guan and Ge kilns, however, its hidden patterns such as orange peel, safflower and blue-and-white, scattered layer upon layer, are attractively fresh and eye-catching. The Yuan dynasty presentation ware made in Shufu prefecture (Jingdezhen) may also be collected. As to the blue-and-white bowls with the finely delineated mark of the Yongle period together with the grape-patterned five-colored bowls of the Chenghua period and others of pure white with the thinness of glass, all are nowadays extremely expensive but in fact of no great elegance.

The finest examples of carving and inscription are from the Song dynasty. The preoccupation of the vulgar with pieces with bodies of silver or gold is utterly laughable since the wonder of carving lies in the proficiency of a technique where the skill is not apparent, as well as the use of the brightest vermilion and a lacquer that is thick, hard and without cracks. In Song pieces, the carving of landscapes, buildings, people and birds and beasts are magnificent; no more can be said. In the Yuan dynasty, Zhang Cheng and Yang Mao were renowned for a time for their skill while in the present dynasty the products of the Orchard Yard may not quite achieve the skill of the Song dynasty but are exquisite nevertheless. In the carving of household utensils the foremost in the Song dynasty was Zhan Cheng. Xia Baiyan achieved a name in the present dynasty and his work was much esteemed by the imperial family during the Xuande period. In the land of Wu, He Si, Li Wenfu and Lu Zigang were master craftsmen in succession, their best work being in white jade, amber, crystal and agate¹; work in bamboo or wood is of no value. The carving of fruit stones although an extremely intricate exercise of skill is, in the end, a heterodox practice.

---

1 *Bi*, this is jadeite.

CHAPTER EIGHT
DRESS AND ORNAMENTS

The mode of dress must be suited to the times. People of my generation cannot dress in rags yet neither can they bedeck themselves in jewelry. One should wear hemp in the summer and furs in winter and clothing should be both refined and modest. In the city one should adopt the style of the scholar and in the countryside the appearance of a hermit. If one were to don garish clothing and compete with the rich and wealthy, how could that properly accord with the ideal of the pleasing garb of the gentleman poet?

The costume of the Han dynasty consisted of a cicada patterned headdress and red robe with a crossover collar, over which was worn a white circular collar with a square suspended ornament, a jade ornamented girdle and red boots. The cap and gown belong to the Sui dynasty and the gauze hat and round collar are the mark of the Tang dynasty. Song dynasty costume consisted of a brimmed hat and long gown or skirt-jacket and long cap or *fujin* (a type of cap, loosely resembling the mediaeval European toque or chaperon, made from a width of silk wrapped into a shape on the head and worn with the ends draping the shoulders).

Fig. 125 *Listening to the* Qin *(detail)*
Zhao Ji
Ink and color on silk
Height 147.2 cm × Width 51.3 cm
Palace Museum, Beijing

The painting depicts nobility and literary gentry listening to the *qin*. The host, wearing a black gown and a cap sits upright between his guests playing the *qin* with utter concentration. The two guests seated on stone drums in the foreground, one on the left in a green gown and the other on the right in a red gown, sit as if intoxicated by the sound of the instrument. They are both dressed in full-sleeved long gowns, according to Wen Zhenheng, typical of a type of Song costume.

The cap ornamented with jade, round collars, hats and waist girdles are of the Yuan dynasty and the square cap and round collar are of this (Ming) dynasty. All these are historical modes of dress and are not to be taken lightly.

Daoist Costume

Daoist costume consists of a long robe of white fabric extended by a border of black cloth, or a long gown of tea-colored material edged in black. There is also a "moon" robe which when spread on the ground resembles the shape of the moon and when worn looks like a coat of crane's feathers. Both of these are essential to the practice of seated Zen, for travel by donkey or horse and for protection against snow and cold.

Zen Costume

The Zen robe is made of felt commonly called *suohala*, a foreign word not easy to understand. It resembles drooping strands of wool, as thick as felt and hardwearing. It comes from the Western Regions. I hear it is very expensive there.

Quilts and Coverings

Quilts are made of a colored serge material and also come from the Western Regions. The material is just over one *chi* (about 30 cm) wide and is much the same as *suohala* felt but is not closely woven or thick. Next is a hardwearing silk from Shandong and although its flower and water pattern and purple and white brocades look well, they are not particularly elegant. Large quilts for use during the winter may be made from purple patterned material. There are others bearing pictures of the one hundred butterflies, known as "butterfly dreams." These are vulgar. The ancients used reeds and rushes as a bed covering. These are no longer made.

Mattresses

In the capital they have folding mattresses, rather like a screen in shape, which measure more than a *zhang* (about 3 meters) in length when extended, but measure only a little over two *chi* (about 60 cm) in length and three to four *cun* (about 9–12 cm) thick when packed up. They are made of brocade, and stuffed with tiger whisker grass (*Juncus effusus*) from which lamp wicks are made. They are elegant indeed. The cushions and mattresses for chairs and couches are made from ancient brocade. When the brocade is worn out it may be used for mounting scrolls.

Woolen Rugs

These come from Shaanxi and Gansu. The red is like coral but they are not suitable to the refined household. The natural-colored ones are the best and may be used to replace mats in the winter. Mattresses of fox fur and sable are difficult to obtain but they are the warmest and most comfortable. Felt is not to be used but dark felt may be placed beneath the paper when writing large characters.

Curtains and Nets

In the winter, curtains may be made of Shandong silk or thick purple pattered material.

Fig. 126   Cap in Amber for Securing the Hair
Height 3.7 cm × Width 6.7 cm × Depth back to front 3.2 cm
Round topped gold hairpins, length 7 cm
Recovered in 1977 from the 12th year of Zhengde (1517) tomb of Xu Fu (1450–1517) at Bancang outside the Taiping Gate in Nanjing
Nanjing Museum

In ancient China men wore their hair tied back and caps were used for securing it. They were also a class of head ornament. They first appeared during the Five dynasties and gradually came into more general use after the Song dynasty and reached the height of popularity in the Ming dynasty. This cap is carved from a piece of semi-transparent reddish gold amber with the addition of two gold hairpins. It takes the form of a half-moon with the back higher than the front. Five vertical ridges support a raised edge in the upper part. A small hole on either side takes a hairpin to secure the hair.

Paper curtains and curtains of fine silk are vulgar and brocade or white silk curtains are items for the women's quarters. In the summer, curtains are made of abaca hemp (*Musa textilis*) but it is difficult to obtain. In the land of Wu, curtains may also be made from blue-green silk gauze or decorated cloth flags. Some curtains are made from silk, others are painted with landscapes and plum blossom in ink: though these strive for elegance, they may descend into vulgarity. There are also large curtains known as "skyfillers" within which one

Fig. 127   *Court Ladies with Fans* (detail)
This detail comes from the third section of the scroll and is entitled "Adjusting the hair in front of a mirror." Two figures stand opposite each other, the one on the right is an imperial concubine who seems to have just woken up and is combing her hair in the mirror held by the figure on the left who is wearing men's clothing. She/he wears a Tang head cloth, a long red gown and a loosely tied waist sash. The two tails of the head cloth tied behind the head can be distinctly seen.

Fig. 128 Portrait of a Ming Personage
Princeton University

The subject of this painting is wearing a long cap and a gown. A long cap means that the whole width of it is used to bind the head, thus enveloping the hair from the forehead back. The head cloth is tied tightly and the remaining material hangs naturally down the back, usually to shoulder level. This is the attire of the refined, much seen amongst scholar officials.

Fig. 129 *On the River During the Qingming Festival* (detail)
Zhang Zeduan (Northern Song dynasty)
Ink and color on silk
Height 24.8 cm × Length 528 cm
Palace Museum, Beijing

The detail is a scene from the last section of the scroll showing a number of people including a middle-aged man of refined appearance mounted on a white horse, clasping a whip and wearing a rain hat and a round-collared gown that reaches the ground. His leisurely expression suggests that he is obviously the master of this group. Rain hats were generally of this shape and were a frequently encountered means of protecting the head against wind, rain, and sun.

may sit or lie in the summer, equipped with tables, couches, chests and stands, which, although agreeable, are not elegantly antique. In a small studio in the winter, blue-green or purple cloth curtains may be hung over the window bars.

fashionable "hanging cloud" style (flat and square on top and hanging to the shoulders at the back) is vulgar in the extreme and possibly an individual style. The long cap (fig. 128) is the most ancient but is inconvenient to wear.

Formal Headwear

Amongst formal headwear, the "crown of iron" is the most ancient followed by headwear decorated with rhinoceros horn, jade and amber (fig. 126). Agarwood and gourds are next and the least ancient are the joints between the sections of bamboo, and burl wood. There are but two styles, that of the moon on its side (a horizontal crescent) and that of scholars and officials. The rest are unsuitable.

Head Cloths

The Tang dynasty head cloth is not far removed from that of the Han dynasty (the Tang dynasty head cloth had two tails hung down at the back) (fig. 127). The presently

Rain Hats (fig. 129)

The best are made of woven cane, two *chi* four *cun* across (a diameter of about 72 cm) with a stitched brim of black silk, which will protect from wind and sun when traveling in the hills. There are also hats made from leaves and from feathers but these are local products and not for everyday use.

Boots

For winter use, boots woven from a layer of hemp or rice straw over reeds are most suited and keep the feet warm. In the summer, only coir shoes from Wenzhou are any good, though if there are styles of wooden-soled waterproof boots that are not vulgar they may be of help in climbing hills or crossing streams.

CHAPTER NINE
BOATS AND CARRIAGES

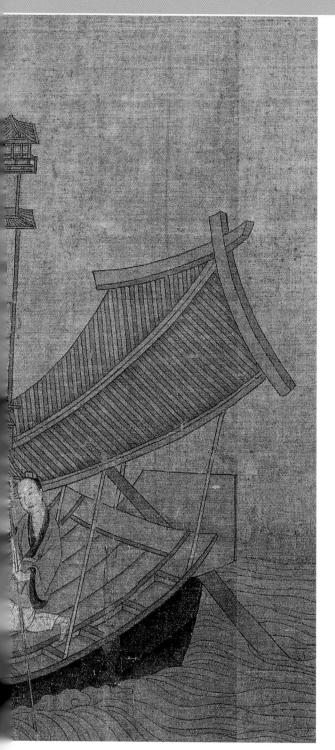

Boats are habituated to water and, from the poop deck of a barge to the bow of a warship, are beyond the purse of the impecunious scholar. Nor can the scholar take his ease in a small boat that resembles a dragonfly or grasshopper. Windows and railings are important, a boat should be as dignified as a proper residence and all must be suitable, both the furnishings within and the entertainment without. Boats may be used for welcoming and bidding farewell and to ease the atmosphere of parting; they may be used for traveling abroad through hills and water and for contemplative thoughts of stillness and seclusion; for expeditions to the snow and for returning loaded with the moon[1] and for the expression of a refined demeanor; for the enjoyment of the fragrance of an early morning in spring; or of the sight of the beauty of women gathering lotus flowers or of listening to the sound of the midnight song[2]; or for the sound of singing and dancing

---

1 There are romantic poetic references to fishermen and others who having been out in a boat overnight returned "loaded with the moon" rather than fish.
2 Probably the poem by Li Bai (701–762) entitled *A Midnight Song of Wu*.

Fig. 130 Copy of Gu Kaizhi's *Verses on the Nymph of the Luo River* (detail)

Anon. (Song dynasty)
Ink and color on silk
Height 27.1 cm × Length 572.8 cm
Palace Museum, Beijing

This painting was created on the basis of Cao Zhi's (192–232) verses about the nymph of the Luo River. The painting depicts his chance encounter with the nymph on the banks of the river. This painting is a detail and depicts a small boat with railings and windows just as the one described by Wen Zhenheng, just like a small house, his ideal boat.

Fig. 131 *A Willow Boat on the West Lake* (detail)
Xia Gui
Ink and color on silk
Height 107.2 cm × Width 59.3 cm
Palace Museum, Taibei

The painting depicts a scene of some elegance on
the shore of the West Lake near Hangzhou. The
dikes, the lakeside willows and thatched huts, as
well as the small bays of the lake, are thronged with
fishing vessels and small, visiting leisure craft, and
a light air of dampness seems to hit one in the face.
In the detail above two figures carried in litters
are to be seen enjoying an outing by the hills and
water and taking in the lake's spring atmosphere.
In the beginning, the shoulder carriage consisted of
two long poles with a chair for seating a person in
between them and no cover. Thereafter, the four
sides of the chair gradually developed into protective
covers, rather like the later carriage in shape.

in midstream. All these are amongst the
agreeable occasions of life.

For help in ascending hills, the most
convenient conveyance is a wicker sedan
chair. As long as it is up-to-date it is well
able to travel far and wide, uphill and down.
Must it be that one has to move in a carriage
ornamented with pearls and jade, inlaid with
gold cowrie shells, equipped with woolen rugs
woven with scenes of many colors, furnished
with grass mats, decorated with tassels, with
ornamented wheels and shafts and adorned
with reins of leather and a bell that sounds like
the call of a phoenix, before it can be deemed
suitable for traveling the highways and byways
of the empire?

Sedan Chairs

The "shoulder carriage" of today is the "curtained carriage" of the ancients (fig. 131). However, the ancients used oxen and horses whereas today we use men to convey us. Truly this is unsuited to a gentleman. The carriages of Fujian and Guangdong are light, convenient and elegant in construction. In Chu (present-day Henan and Hubei) they have excellent sedan chairs with shoulder poles of cane. The present-day twisted rattan sedan chairs produced in Jinling (present-day Nanjing) are vulgar in the extreme.

Bamboo Chairs

Where there are no aids to traveling in the hills one cannot be without a bamboo chair. The kind made in Wulin (present-day Hangzhou) has a seat and a footrest bound into a net of rope so that up and down and over hill and dale one feels as if on level ground. This is very agreeable but there is no protection from the wind and rain. There is a type equipped with a frame upon which a canopy may be mounted. This is not an elegant sight.

Flat-Bottomed Barges

The flat-bottomed barge is much like a rowing boat in shape though the bottom is flat. It is just over three *zhang* in length (about 9 meters) and five *chi* (about 1.5 meters) across at the bow. It is divided into four cabins. The center cabin will accommodate host and guests, six people in all, and is furnished with tables and benches, brush stands, vessels for warming wine, cooking cauldrons, wine vessels, flower pots and so on, the more delicate the better. The forecabin will accommodate a total of four boys or servants and is equipped with wine pots, tea stoves and other tea making utensils. The aft cabin is separated into two by planking and has a small passageway for entering and leaving. A couch and low table may be set up in the center of the vessel. A plank may be placed on top of a small cupboard upon which may be placed calligraphy scrolls, brush, inkstones and so forth. A clothes chest and chamber pot may be placed beneath the couch. The sails are not made from grass matting but are battened. There are no railings either side but there are silken cloth screens as protection against the sun instead. When the sun is not shining, the screens are raised and secured with a tie and not a hook (fig. 132). Other types of vessel,

Fig. 132 *Parting at Xunyang* (detail)
Qiu Ying
Ink and color on paper
Height 33.7 cm × Length 400.7 cm
Nelson Atkins Museum of Art, Kansas City

The Tang dynasty poet Bai Juyi's poem *Song of the Pipa Player* describes him bidding farewell to a guest at the head of the Xunyang River. The painting is based on the spirit of the poem. Beyond the trees and undergrowth two boats are moored side by side, one of them broad and handsome with several cabins, an awning above and curtains at the four sides. Several people are seated round a table in the cabin and a young servant busies himself next door. There are differences with the boat described by Wen Zhenheng but overall they are much the same; one can see how the literati disported themselves aboard a boat.

Fig. 133 *Poling a Boat in the Shadow of the Pines in Late Evening*

Zhao Mengfu
Blue-and-green on silk
Height 152.6 cm ×
Width 79 cm
Palace Museum, Taibei

It is evening and a scholar sits in a small boat resting under the pine trees and gazing peacefully forwards. A young boy sits at the stern of the boat propelling it with an oar or paddle. One can see that the boat has a blue awning and that the sides of the boat have been extended by railings. The awning is supported by two poles at the bow and the painting is remarkably similar to Wen Zhenheng's description. It is sufficiently detailed to show the author's partiality for the life of the literati in previous dynasties as well as for "ancient design and construction."

such as tower ships and two vessels lashed together proceeding alongside each other, are vulgar.

Small Boats

Small boats or punts measure slightly more than one *zhang* in length (about 3 meters) and three *chi* in width (about 90 cm) and occupy pools and ponds, though at times they may be rowed in midstream or moored at a bank beneath the shade of willows, where with fishing rod and line in hand one may murmur verses of the wind and moon (fig. 133). Small

Fig. 134 *Fishing at the Mouth of a Stream*
Attributed to Xia Gui
Ink and color on silk
Height 23.2 cm × Width 23.8 cm
Metropolitan Museum of Art, New York

Employing great economy of line the artist has sketched a figure fishing quietly from a boat at the mouth of a stream. The painting quietly emits an ambience of propitious tranquility that is absolutely in keeping with the scholar's inner world.

boats may have an awning of blue cloth, a footway on either side with two bamboo poles forward rigged to two bollards at the stern, and a boy to row the boat (fig. 134).

CHAPTER TEN
PLACING AND ARRANGEMENT

Methods of placing differ as between elaborate and simple and as between winter and summer. There is a method suitable for spacious halls and broad pavilions and another suitable for quiet rooms and secluded chambers. Even calligraphy and books, bronze vessels and the like must be arranged appropriately before they can achieve the beauty of a painting. The single couch and table in the artist Ni Zan's Studio of Rare Treasures, set amongst trees and rocks, are enough to bring to mind his grace and style and send a shiver of delight through body and soul. Thus it is that on entering the abode of a gentleman scholar one senses a feeling of elegant superiority that extinguishes vulgarity. If, however, pigs and chickens are kept in the entrance hall and yet the inner court is extravagantly appointed for watering plants and washing stones, then it would be better by far just to have tables deep in dust surrounded by four plain walls, so achieving a kind of distinguished desolation.

Fig. 135 *Mountain Retreat of the Purple Fungus*
Ni Zan
Ink on paper
Height 80.5 cm × Width 34.8 cm
Palace Museum, Taibei

A huge rock stands on a slope amidst a number of different kinds of tree and a thatched bower has been built overlooking the water. Water separates us from the distant view where a range of mountains is clearly visible. The bower is absolutely empty; nevertheless, it expresses the simplicity and breadth of mind and elegant freedom from vulgarity of the literati.

Fig. 136 *At Study in the Hill Studio* (detail)

Liu Songnian
Ink and color on silk
Height 24.3 cm × Width 24 cm
Palace Museum, Taibei

This painting depicts the life of ease to which the literary gentry aspired. Beneath the shade of the pines and in a gentle breeze stands a small building containing stools, tables, and chairs and books. Literary impedimenta are scattered on the table. Outside one can hear the sound of a boy servant sweeping up the leaves; it is a scene of relaxed tranquility. What contentment is to be found in sitting at one's desk opening scrolls, looking at paintings and examining calligraphy!

Writing Tables

A writing table in natural form may be placed on the left of a room, facing east though in order to avoid sunshine and draughts it should not be too close to a window (fig. 136). On it should be placed one antique inkstone, one brushpot, one ink palette, one small water basin and one further inkstone in the form of a mountain. The ancients placed inkstones on the left so that the reflection from the ink should not dazzle the eye, making writing by lamplight more convenient. Best of all, there should also be a book-weight rule and a paperweight, both polished frequently until they gleam.

Seating

Zen chairs and couches of speckled bamboo may be used for seating. In winter they may be adorned with antique brocade or a tiger skin.

Chairs, Couches, Screens and Stands

A studio should contain only four chairs and a single couch. Other furnishings such as altars to the Buddha, short couches, low tables and round or semicircular tables may be added but ranging chairs against a wall should be avoided and there should be only one screen. There may be bookcases and chests to take books and histories but it is not well to indulge in the disorder of a bookshop (fig. 137).

Hanging Paintings

Paintings should be hung high and only one in a studio. It is extremely vulgar to hang paintings on opposite walls. Long paintings may be hung high on a wall but should not be hung crooked with the aid of a bamboo prop①. Curious stones or in season, *penjing* may be placed on a painting table. Vermilion and red lacquer stands are to be avoided. Large horizontal scrolls are suitable for a hall but small examples of scenery and flowers-and-birds for a studio. Single strips, fan leaves, square paintings and hanging screens (screen panels stuck or inset into a frame for hanging) are not an attractive sight. If paintings do not match their surroundings, the effect is ridiculous.

① The use of a bamboo crosspiece upon which to drape a section of a painting when it is too long.

Fig. 137 *Passing the Summer*
Liu Guandao (Yuan dynasty)
Ink and color on silk
Height 30.5 cm × Length 71.1 cm
Nelson Atkins Museum of Art, Kansas City

Banana trees, parasol trees, and bamboo grow in the courtyard. On the left there is a couch on which a reclining figure is taking the breeze. Immediately behind him there is a *qin* and on the table behind the couch there is an assortment of calligraphy scrolls, inkstones and tea bowls. One can see that the master of this establishment is a stylish member of the literati. There is a natural reality about the figure and an air of elegant tranquility about the painting.

Displaying Incense Burners

A small Japanese-made square table may be placed upon an ordinary everyday table and a single incense burner may be placed upon that, together with a large box containing fresh and matured incense and two small boxes, one containing agarwood incense and the other incense briquettes, as well as a vase for chopsticks. Two burners may not be used in a studio nor should a burner be placed next to a picture or vases and boxes placed opposite each other. Porcelain burners may be used during the summer and bronze in winter.

The Placing of Vases

Vases may be placed upon large or small Japanese tables according to their size, bronze vases in winter and spring and porcelain in summer and autumn. Halls are suited to large vases and studios to small ones. Pottery and bronze vases are precious, silver and gold vulgar, vases with ears or handles are to be avoided as are vases in pairs. Slender flowers are suitable, elaborate and profuse bunches are not. Where a single stem is used, the choice should be one of unique elegance and appearance; where two stems are used they should be of different lengths and confined to just one or two varieties, too many and it will look like a tavern, though in autumn one need not be so particular about the number of varieties in small vases. One should not close the shutters and burn incense where flowers are displayed since they wither when touched by smoke; narcissi are very sensitive in this respect. Flowers may not be placed on painting tables (fig. 138).

Small Chambers

It is not fitting to have a multitude of couches and tables in a small room but one may have an ancient narrow-bordered book table furnished with an inkstone, an incense box, and a small incense burner; all these are small and elegant. There may also be a small stone table upon which to place tea bowls and utensils, and a small couch upon which to recline or lie or sit in a Buddha-like posture. There is no need for pictures though some display ancient and curious stones or small cabinets with gilded Buddhas; all this may be allowed.

Bedchambers

Although ceilings and planked flooring may be vulgar they may be used in a bedchamber because of the need to keep dry and prevent damp, but in no case should colored paintings or oil paint be present. A sleeping couch may be installed on the south side of the room with a space of half a room behind it, inaccessible to people but where warming pans or brazier perfume lids, clotheshorses, washbasins, trunks and reading lamps may be stored. A low table with nothing on it may be placed in front of the couch together with two square stools and a small cabinet for aromatic herbs for the braziers, as well as other curios. A chamber should have an elegant purity of atmosphere. Once tinged with luxury it becomes like a lady's bedchamber, no place for the remote and lofty musings of the reclusive scholar. There should also be a recess in the wall to take a bed suitable for nocturnal conversation (the practice of lying side by side and reminiscing through the night) with a drawer beneath to store boots and stockings. One should not grow too many plants in the courtyard, just a few well-loved varieties with one rare stem set amongst them, accompanied by Lingbi stones and Ying stones.

Pavilions and Waterside Pavilions

Pavilions and pavilions by water offer no protection from wind and rain and are unsuitable for the display of items of excellence. At the same time, items of vulgar

taste are unbearable so one should use simple and natural old lacquer, square and with sturdy feet, for a pavilion. For sitting outside in the open one may use low flat stones dredged from a lake and scattered here and there. One should not use stone or tile blocks or pillars. In particular, one should not place vermilion lacquer stands on the top of bricks from the Guan Kiln.

Opening Rooms to the Outside

In high summer it is fitting to remove windows and window bars and, with the protection from the sun of the Chinese parasol trees in front and bamboo at the back, place a large wooden table in the center of

Fig. 138 *A Song Personage*
Anon. (Song dynasty)
Ink and color on silk
Height 29 cm × Width 27.8 cm
Palace Museum, Taibei

A figure is seated on a couch as if just about take up a brush and commence writing. A *qin*, chess pieces, calligraphy, and paintings are set out on the furniture around him. A portrait hangs on the screen standing behind the couch. A stone stands in front of the couch with a flowerpot on top containing two different kinds of flowers, set off by leaves. This painting demonstrates the interest of the generally leisurely way in which the literati of the past hung their pictures, arranged flowers and burned incense.

the room with an unscreened long couch on either side. There is no need to hang any scrolls as they can be damaged by the summer

Fig. 139 "Scenes of Taking the Breeze" from *Four Landscapes*

Liu Songnian
Ink and color on silk
Height 40 cm × Length 69 cm
Palace Museum, Beijing

This scroll is divided into four, each section depicting the scenery of one of the four seasons. The top section illustrates taking the breeze in summer and illustrates the shady trees round the building and the jade-like lotus plants that dot the water surrounding the waterside pavilion. The skill of the artist's brush has meticulously caught the fine construction of the courtyard and water pavilion.

The left-hand detail below shows how, although the building is open on all four sides, a sense of coolness suddenly sweeps in from the heavy shade of the green trees. A figure sits in a broad chair with either a table or couch at his side and the space in front of the court is occupied by strange rocks. The right-hand detail below shows a pavilion on the water attached to the main building. A stone table is vaguely visible within. These details afford a glimpse and give a sense of the leisured life of the literati.

Fig. 140 Gilded Bronze of the Seated
Sakyamuni Buddha

Ming dynasty, Yongle period
Height 19.2 cm, width 13.2 cm
Liaoning Provincial Museum

In this statue the eyes are un-slanted and
the eyebrows slender, giving a general
expression of calm. A *kassaya* is draped
across the left shoulder of the figure,
which is seated on a lotus throne.
The statue is both graceful and yet
luxurious in style.

sunlight, moreover, since the
wall space has been opened
up there is nowhere for
them to hang. A couch
of speckled bamboo may
be placed at the north
window where one may
recline upon a bamboo
mat. One should choose
a large inkstone, a blue-
green water bowl and
large bronze vessels to put on the table. One
or two pots of orchids can be placed next to
a long table while there is no objection to an
arrangement of *penjing* of strange peaks and
elegantly ancient trees, sparkling streams and

white stones. The room may be hung
with curtains of speckled bamboo.
To see it is to enter the realm of
delight (fig. 139).

Buddha Chamber or Chapel

The superior Buddha chamber
is furnished with a thickly
gilded small statue of
the Buddha made in
Tibet and of benevolent
aspect and imposing
demeanor (fig. 140).
Alternatively, a Song
or Yuan dynasty plain
unrobed statuette of
Guanyin on an ancient
lacquer altar may be installed. If a set of
statues representing the Buddhist deities
called a "hall" has been installed together with
a small vermilion lacquer altar, then this is
more suited to the abode of a monk than to
the residence of a gentleman. It is excellent to
have an ancient stone statue that was found by
a cave beneath towering pines. Flowers may
be placed on a table in an ancient narrow-
stemmed vase with a water bowl for pouring
water and a small stone cauldron for burning
impressed incense tablets. Stone lanterns for
use at night, bells, chimes, banners, tables and
couches should all be set out in order, but
daintiness is to be avoided. Bells and chimes
should not be placed together. An ancient
Japanese-made lacquer chest for storing
sutras may be used to contain the Buddhist
scriptures. A platform for offerings of food,
a banner pole, and a stone pillar carved with
the names of the Buddha, or Buddhist texts
set on an ancient stone lotus base carved with
lotus flowers, may be erected in the courtyard.
Several varieties of plants may be grown round
the pillar and the stone must be ancient or at
least washed by water to give the appearance
of antiquity.

南園昨夜雨肥勝
大官羊瓮民銷
金懷何自得一當
沈周 瓶

Fig. 141 *Vegetables*
Shen Zhou
Ink on paper
Height 92.3 cm × Width 31.7 cm
Palace Museum, Taibei

The painting depicts a cabbage.
Its stems are shown in fine
outline with the remainder filled
in with a light wash. Leaves are
treated in an uneven black wash
contrasted with the moss on the
slope. The painting may appear
both simple and concise but
it is suffused with the spirit of
the brushwork. The subject of
this painting is quite ordinary,
nevertheless, it enshrines the
literati ethos of "preserving
the truth of the evanescent
and seeing the poverty in
permanence."

CHAPTER ELEVEN
FRUIT AND VEGETABLES

When Lord Meng (?–279 BC) of the state of Qi during the period of the Warring States period entertained guests, the upper guests ate meat, the middle guests ate fish and the lower guests ate fruit and vegetables; from this sprang the power of the ancients. My generation praises the purity of fungus and cinnamon but will not eat chrysanthemum heads or *baizhu* (*Atractylodes macrocephala*), or try plants and grasses, yet they satisfy their appetite by gorging on flesh and wine; this may well be called an insult to the simple life of the scholar. The ancients offered waterclover (*Marsilea quadrifolia*) and artemisia (*Artemisia stelleriana*) and presented vegetables and bamboo shoots as a delicacy, thus it is that the flavors of the hills and the plants of the wild must be raised and cultivated to assist in daytime converse and evening drinking. Food containers and vessels for heating wine should be both elegant and delicate with no trace of the market stall. One should collect the best wines as well as the delicacies of land and sea, such as dried venison or lychee fruit that appeal both to tongue and eye and not merely to a pair of chopsticks and a watering mouth.

Sour Cherry

The ancients used to call the sour cherry (fig. 142) (*Prunus pseudocerasus*) the "vermilion cherry" (*zhutao*) or "heroic cherry" (*yingtao*). It is much taken by birds, a habit referred to in the *Book of Rites*. When contained in a white bowl it is exquisite in both color and flavor. In the courtesans' quarter of the Southern Capital (Nanjing) they have a very good sour cherry preserve to which rugosa rose leaves are added for flavor. It is extremely expensive.

Fig. 142 *Orioles on a Sour Cherry Tree*
Anon. (Song dynasty)
Ink and color on silk
Height 12.1 cm × Length 26.1 cm
Shanghai Museum
This painting is filled with the life and interest of each tender luscious fresh red sour cherry. Each of the two yellow orioles on the tree adopts a different but realistic posture.

Fig. 143   Flat Peach

Fig. 144   Citron

Peach, Chinese Plum, Plum *Mei* (*Armeniaca mume*) and Apricot

Peach trees come to fruit quickly so that as the proverb says, even the elderly may plant a peach tree and expect to live to see it bear fruit. Its varieties include the *Prunus communis*, the inkstick peach (*motao*), the golden peach (*jintao*), a peach with a pointed protrusion and the flat peaches (*Prunus persica var. compressa*) (fig. 143); cooked in honey these are delicious. Plums rank below peaches, there are two varieties, one dusky green in color and the other with a yellow skin, called yellow nun. There is another variety known as "son of Jia Qing" (*jiaqing zi*) that has a slightly sour taste. Northerners do not distinguish between plum *mei* and apricots until they are ripe. Plum *mei* grafted on to apricot stock are known as *xingmei* (*Prunus mume var. bungo*), another kind is *xiaomei* (*Prunus mume var. microcarpa*) that dissolves in the mouth and is both crisp and delicious. Even though it is just an ordinary variety it can quench thirst and raise the spirits and has a quality of its own.

Tangerine and Orange

The tangerine is a "slave fruit" that supplies both food and profit. There are green tangerines (*Citrus tangrina*), gold tangerines (*Citrus microcarpa*), honey tangerines and flat tangerines, all from Dongting (two hills, east and west, bordering Lake Taihu near Suzhou). There is a further variety of similar color and flavor grown in Fujian and known as "lacquer dish red" that is even better. Thin-skinned tangerines from Quzhou (*Citrus erythrosa*) are good as well but are difficult to obtain in any quantity. Hill folk make unripe fallen tangerines into medicine, the pickled kind being the best. Yellow oranges may be chopped up and used as a seasoning called "golden shred" by the ancients. Chopped seasoning made by the same method today is known as "common flavoring."

Large Tangerine

Large tangerines (*gan*) are grown on the east and west hills at Dongting and are sweet in taste. The tangerines from Xinzhuang (now in Huqiu District of Suzhou in Jiangsu Province) have no juice and have to be cut with a knife before eating. There is another kind with a thick skin called *Citrus poonensis* that is also good. Small ones are called golden tangerines (*Fortunella crassifolia*) and round ones "round beans" (*Fortunella hindsii*).

Citron

Citrons (*Citrus medica*) are the size of a bowl and have a strong fragrance and are very popular amongst the people of the land of Wu. Presented in a porcelain bowl with the pith removed and mixed with white sugar they can be made into soup to be drunk to quench thirst after taking wine. There is another variety with a slightly thicker skin and with an even stronger fragrance (fig. 144).

Loquat

The best loquats (*Eriobotrya japonica*) are those with a single stone, the stem and leaves are both attractive. They are also (erroneously) known as *kuandonghua*[①], coltsfoot (*Tussilago farfara*). When dried and served in a fruit box they resemble yellow gold and have a fine scent (fig. 145).

① The confusion over identification arose because both the loquat and coltsfoot blossom in the snow. However, they are completely different.

Bayberry

Bayberries are among the best fruit of the land of Wu and are more or less as well known as lychee fruit. The best come from Guangfu Hill (now on the western outskirts of Suzhou) where people use lacquer bowls to hold them, their color matching the lacquer. Just twenty bayberries weigh one *jin* (about half a kilogram) and are of rare fragrance. They ripen in high summer but cannot be transported far, so that those who have a taste for them either have them delivered by fast boat or travel themselves by boat to taste them. Bayberries grown on other hills are sour and lack the

Fig. 145 *Bird with Loquats*
Anon. (Song dynasty)
Ink and color on silk
Height 26.9 cm × Width 27.2 cm
Palace Museum, Beijing

It is May in the south of China and ripe, golden loquats look exceptionally enticing in the summer sun. A small bird perches on a branch and is about to take a peck at the fruit. The loquats are shaded in three different colors. It is almost as if one can smell their sweet fragrance and even the navel of each fruit is delineated in every detail with exquisitely meticulous brush strokes.

purple coloring. Some people dip them in heated wine, the color does not change but the taste is less strong. When pickled in honey both color and taste are foul (fig. 146).

Fig. 146 Bayberry

Fig. 147   Lychee

Grape

There are two kinds of grape: white and purple. The white variety is known as "white crystal" and does not taste quite as good as the purple kind.

Lychee

Although lychees are not grown in the land of Wu, they are a well-known fruit and very popular. The story of the "gallop through the red dust[1]" to fetch lychees on behalf of the Imperial Concubine Yang Guifei is not necessarily proof that she was thoughtless. There are also lychees that have been pickled in honey, white in color though the skin has turned red. There is also the saying "a skin of red silk and white jade," which is just a figment of the popular imagination (fig. 147). Longan fruit (*Dimocarpus longan*), known as the lychee's slave (it reaches the market just as the lychee departs), is not as delicious as the lychee and has fewer varieties, though it is more expensive.

Date

There are many varieties of date. The taste of the small-stoned red date is particularly sweet. The price of preserved dates from Jinling (Nanjing) and southern dates from Zhejiang is extremely high (fig. 148).

Fig. 148   Date

Pear

There are two kinds of pear: one with plump spreading petals that has sweet tasting fruit and the other lesser, wrinkled kind with a sour taste. The two are easily distinguishable. There is a kind from Shandong that is as large as a squash and very crisp in taste, it dissolves in the mouth and can reduce an excess of phlegm.

Chestnut

When the poet Du Fu (712–770) was in the land of Shu (part of present-day Sichuan Province), he existed by picking chestnuts; and for the hill folk of Shu there were only chestnuts to stave off poverty. Chestnuts from the hills of the land of Wu are exceptionally small but wind-dried they taste delicious. Chestnuts from Wuxing are transported by stream and river and spoil easily but are good roasted.

Chestnuts eaten with olives are known as "plum blossom preserve" since in the mouth they taste of plum blossom, though in fact it is not absolutely so (fig. 149).

Fig. 149   Chestnut

Ginkgo Fruit

The leaves of the ginkgo tree resemble the webbed feet of a duck and are thus called "duck's feet." The leaves of the male tree are shaped like a three-leaved fan, whereas those of the female are two-leaved in shape (fig. 150). They are grown in orchards and gardens, though the fruit may not be sufficient (fig. 151). The first green of the leaves is very attractive. In the land of Wu, Buddhist temples abound with luxuriantly spreading gingko trees of huge girth, worthy to be called trees of quality.

Fig. 150   Ginkgo Leaves

Fig. 151   Ginkgo Fruit

Persimmon

Persimmons have seven superior characteristics: longevity, shade, absence of birds, absence of insects, attractive leaves after frost, excellent fruit and leaves that are thick and hard at leaf fall. There is another variety called "lantern persimmon," small and delicate and without a kernel, which tastes even better. There are people who say that after three seasons persimmons will no longer fruit. I do not know whether this is true or not (fig. 152).

Fig. 152   Persimmon

Crab Apple

Crab apples (*Malus asiatica*) are known as "nai" (*Malus pumila var. astracanica*) in the North West and everybody makes them into crab apple preserve. They are what is known today as *pinpo* fruit. They are best eaten raw. Particularly sweet, they smell fresh. In the land of Wu they are called "Flower Red," "Birds of the Forest," or "Bird Visitors." They are a little smaller than *nai* with attractive flowers.

Water Caltrop

The two-horned variety of the water caltrop (*Trapa bicornis*) is called *ling* and the four-horned variety is called *ji* (*Trapa maximowiczii*). In the land of Wu they grow in lakes and domestic ponds. There are two kinds, blue-green and red. The red kind ripens the earliest and is called the "water red caltrop," (fig. 153) the slightly larger and later red kind is called "wild goose red"; the blue-green kind is called "oriole blue" and the larger blue-green kind is called "wonton *ling*" and has the best flavor; the smallest is called "wild *ling*." There is also a kind called "white sand horn." They are all at their best in the autumn and may be served with haricot beans.

---

1 "Red dust" is also a Buddhist term indicating the snares and delusions of the mundane world.

Fig. 153   Water Caltrop

Foxnut

The flower of the foxnut (*Euryale ferox*) opens during the day and closes at night. In the autumn its ovary takes on the appearance of a chicken's head with the seed inside, hence the common name "chicken bean" (fig. 155). There are two varieties, *jing* and *nuo* (references to kinds of sticky rice); and if it is about the same size as the longan fruit, it has an excellent flavor that is beneficial to health. If it is peeled, pounded and cooked into a paste with sugar it completely loses its original flavor.

Fig. 155   Foxnut Fruit

Watermelon

Watermelons (*Citrullus vulgaris*) are sweet and the ancients believed that eating watermelon rinsed in ice cold water was as good as eating plums treated the same way; it is more than just a vegetable. During a long hot summer, it is indispensable for quenching thirst; it is also effective in curing summer ills.

Siberian Ginseng

Siberian ginseng (*Acanthopanax spinosum*) can energize the body and clear the eyes. The people of the land of Wu pick its buds in early spring and dry them to make a kind of tea with a particularly sweet fragrance and flavor. It also makes a wine that extends longevity.

Fig. 154   Flat White Beans

Flat White Bean

Pure white flat beans (*Lablab purpureus*) are fine flavored and are beneficial to the spleen when taken as medicine. They should be planted on fences and in courtyards in the depth of autumn as a food supply. A considerable measure of dried beans should be stored to meet the needs of the year (fig. 154).

Mushroom

Mushrooms cover the hills after rain, particularly in the spring. After Insects Wake (third of the Twenty-Four Solar Terms) when insects and snakes become active, poisonous mushrooms too are at their most numerous, though hill folk have their ways of recognizing them. The flavor of mushrooms is weaker in the autumn. When dried they may be made into a highly priced tea.

Gourd

There is no single variety of gourd. Poets use them as water containers but they may also be plucked and cooked as a vegetable and are a favorite of hill folk, though the taste is not one to be appreciated by people of status.

Aubergine

Another name for aubergine is *luosu*, it is also known as "Kunlun purple melon." It should be grown and watered alongside amaranth (*Amaranthus gangeticus*). Both plants grow prolifically and taste well when freshly plucked. When Cai Zun (467–523) was governor of Wuxing (the area of Huzhou, Hangzhou and Yixing in present-day Zhejiang) he grew white amaranth (*Amaranthus albus*) and purple aubergines in front of his residence as vegetables for eating. If persons of such rank could do this, how is it that people of my generation lack this sort of flavor?

Taro

Fig. 156 Taro

The ancients raised families on the taro (*Colocasia esculenta*) and there is a saying "a garden of chestnuts and taro is guard against poverty." Thus in a battle against poverty the taro is in the lead. The phrase "with roasted taro hot in my hand I am the equal of the emperor himself" directly expresses an imperial joy and whilst these words may be an exaggeration, eating taro huddled round a stove on a cold night is a delicious experience. There is truth in the description of the taro as the "common man's *lingzhi* mushroom[1]."

Wild Rice

Wild rice (*Zizania caduciflora*) was called "mushroom rice" by the ancients and by its nature is very suited to water; if transplanted

Fig. 158 Wild Rice

each year it does not turn black. It is good for planting in ponds and pools to supplement the deficiencies of orchard and garden (fig. 158).

Yam

The (Chinese) yam (*Dioscorea polystachya*) was originally called "potato medicine." The kind produced in Yuewang east of Loujiang (present-day Taicang in Jiangsu Province) is as thick as an arm, worthy to be called lord of heaven's palm and should be an everyday vegetable food (fig. 157). Seeds (bulbils) gathered in the summer are inedible. Other kinds such as fragrant taro, black taro (*Sagittaria sagittifolia*) and water chestnut (*Eleocharis tuberosa*) are not of the best.

Fig. 157 Yams

Radish and Turnip

The radish, also called "reed turnip" and the turnip, also called "six advantages," are both highly flavored vegetables.

The rest, such as black and white cabbage (*Brassica chinensis*), spinach mustard (*Brassica narinosa*), water plant (*Brasenia schreberi*), celery, fern (*Osmunda japonica*) and bracken (*Pteridium aquilinum*) may be planted by a gardener to supply the table but one should on no account sell them at the market for profit and become a vegetable seller.

---

1 The *lingzhi* mushroom was reputed to have medicinal qualities and was associated with immortality.

CHAPTER TWELVE
INCENSE AND TEA

The benefits of incense and tea are extensive. The hermit, detached from the material world, pondering virtue and the way, may by their use clear the mind and gladden the heart. At dawn and dusk when the spirit falters, they ease the soul and allow one to burst into song. When copying a rubbing by a window during the day, or reciting and conversing to the gestures of a fly whisk, or reading by lamplight at night, they have the capacity to banish sleep. In intimate conversations with grey gowns and red sleeves[1] they can aid passion and inflame ardor. Behind closed shutters on a rainy day or walking after a meal they can rid us of loneliness and vexation. They can quench the thirst and revive the spirits after a drunken banquet, or when talking at night by the window, or whistling in an empty chamber, or playing the *qin* and performing music. The finest   .

___
1 Grey gown, the dress of a slave or servant girl; red sleeve, a singing girl or female entertainer.

Fig. 159 *A Meeting of the Literati* (detail)
Zhao Ji
Ink and color on silk
Height 184.4 cm × Width 123.9 cm
Palace Museum, Taibei

This painting depicts tea tasting at a meeting of members of the literati during the Northern Song dynasty. They are seated for discussion round a table, holding tea bowls and engaging in private conversation. Boy servants are busy round a number of small tables in front of the large table. The small tables are covered with tea bowls and their saucers, etc. A boy servant holds a hot water pot as if about to pour. Another boy holds a long-handled ladle and is about to fill the tea bowls with the tea mixture. A tea stove has been set up alongside with a teapot on top. One can vaguely see the fire in the stove, an indication that water is being boiled.

incense is made from agarwood and the best tea is the *jie* tea from Changxin in Zhejiang and Yixing in Jiangsu. However, there is a skill to preparing them both and only gentlemen of refinement are capable of comprehending their true essence.

Ficus Incense

The incense made from the ficus tree (*Ficus retusa*) is of two kinds, sugarwood (*tangjie*) and gold thread (*jinsi*). Sugarwood is the most valuable and is as black as lacquer and as hard as jade. When sawn open its surface exudes a sugary oil and is most valuable. The gold thread variety is yellow in color and streaked with gold thread and is not as good. This incense cannot be

burned as it has a slightly rank odor. Large pieces of sugarwood can weigh up to 15 or 16 *jin* (about 9.6 kg) and when contained in a carved dish will fill a chamber with fragrance, truly a wonderful substance. Small pieces may be used as fan pendants or prayer beads, which when worn in the summer will ward off evil spirits. Normally the incense is contained in a tin box divided into two compartments, the bottom one containing honey to nurture the incense and the top one the incense itself. The partition between is pierced with several longan fruit-shaped holes so that the flavor of the honey seeps up into the incense, which thus never dries out. Agarwood incense may also be kept in the same way (fig. 160).

Fig. 160 *Listening to the Ruan (detail)*

Li Song (Song dynasty)
Ink and color on silk
Height 177.5 cm × Width 104.5 cm
Palace Museum, Taibei

In the shade of some densely planted trees a scholar sits on a couch, his left leg semi-crossed and a whisk in his hand, listening intently and respectfully to a court lady playing the *ruan* (a four-stringed plucked instrument). Another lady stands at an incense table preparing an incense stove on which to burn incense for the scholar. A table displays an ancient *qin* and other antiques, a demonstration of the elegance of the life led by the literati. Listening to the music of these instruments in a cloud of incense, how could one's heart not be eased?

Dragon Spittle Incense (Ambergris)

In the country of Sumandala (Sumatra) there is an island called Dragon Spittle Island[1] upon which dragons breed and mingle, leaving their sputum in the water, which is then collected as incense. That which floats on the water is the best and that mixed with sand is next. That which is eaten by fish and then expelled in the shape of a dipper is even less good. In Sumandala it is both valuable and expensive.

Agarwood Incense

The substance of agarwood is heavy; the best appears black when split open. Normally its quality is determined by the degree to which it floats or sinks in water. Nevertheless, good "fast fragrance" (*suxiang*—agarwood that has been buried for a long time and turned soft) also sinks in water. Having first heated a piece (of agarwood), transfer the ember to another vessel and then use it to perfume clothes and bedding. I once saw a piece of water-worn agarwood incense about two *cun* in size (about 6 cm) and carved with a pattern of dragons and phoenix in the ancestral temple dedicated by the Ming Emperor Shizong (1507–1567) to his father. It was a Daoist altarpiece and for display only.

Fast Fragrance Agarwood Chips

Commonly called "carp chips," the best are patterned like a pheasant and the denser in quality the better. They are not expensive but there are imitations to beware of.

Anba Incense

Anba incense (made from the oil of the *duying* tree—*Elaeocarpus decipiens*—Japanese blueberry) is very strong and when placed in the sleeves of clothing remains effective for several days. However, it is not suitable for use by itself and should be heated together with agarwood, when it is called "black fragrance." Black fragrance that glows in color, is soft in substance and can be kneaded into pellets is the very best. The "*Anba* biscuits" of the capital made from mixing with other incense is not very good.

Horn Incense

Horn incense (incense produced from the grinding together of other incense ingredients) is commonly known as ivory incense and has a decayed black appearance. When shot through with yellow patterning it is called "ripe yellow," the pure white uncured kind is known as "raw fragrance." It is in common use and one should try and find the best. It does not need to be heated separately but should be placed gently in the burner so that the fragrance drifts out without any smoke or flame.

Sweet Incense

Sweet incense made during the Xuande period has an attractive distant fragrance and comes in a lacquer-black earthen jar with the date of manufacture on the white bottom. The jars with tin caps are the best. "Hibiscus" and "plum blossom" are two varieties. The variety currently made in Beijing is also good.

Yellow and Black Incense Biscuits

These incense biscuits were made by the family of Wu Kezhong, Count Gongshun (dates unknown). The best are the size of a copper coin. The small kind made by incense shops and stamped with all kinds of decorations may be used but they are suitable only for women's quarters and not for a studio.

---

1 This may be a reference to Komodo island, upon which Komodo dragons do congregate and which was already known to the Chinese from the voyages of Zheng He earlier in the Ming dynasty. Ambergris, a product of the sperm whale, is usually washed ashore. Dragon's spittle seems to be a myth.

Anxi[1] Incense

There are many varieties of incense (made from the dried sap of the tree *Styrax benzoin*) known under the name "Anxi incense." The best are "moon dragon," "assembly of immortals," and "swift agarwood." Swift agarwood combined with two other ingredients is very good. The Palace Manufactory produces an incense coil called "hanging dragon" which burns suspended, the frame from which it hangs is very unusual. Other varieties such as "orchid," "ten thousand springs," and "hundred flowers" are useless.

Warm Chamber and Rue

There are two kinds of "warm chamber" incense, yellow and black. "Rue incense[①]" and "short bunch" from the Zhou family residence [the residence of Zhu Su (1361–1425), a

① Rue (*Ruta graveolens*), a perennial shrub of the citrus family. It has woody lower stems with yellow-green flowers, the whole extremely fragrant, its sap when burned may be used to fumigate clothing to rid them of damp.

member of the Ming imperial family] are excellent. However, they are mentioned only for the sake of completeness and are not for use.

Cangzhu (*Atractylodes lancea*)

Cangzhu incense should be burned frequently at the year's end and during the rainy season of early summer. It comes from Jurong (in present-day Jiangsu Province) where the slender stems that grow on Maoshan are the best, though the genuine article is difficult to obtain.

Tea

With ease one can recall several score commentators on the customs and practice of tea drinking. They include Lu Yu (733–804), author of the *Classic of Tea* and Cai Xiang

Fig. 161 *Milling Tea* (detail)
Liu Songnian
Ink and color on silk
Height 44.2 cm × Width 61.9 cm
Palace Museum, Taibei

In the left foreground a servant is milling tea on a tea grinder. The square table at the side is laid with each and every utensil necessary for the preparation of tea. Another servant holds a teapot in his right hand and a tea bowl in his left as if about to make tea. The wind stove beside him is boiling water in a scene of neatness and order that demonstrates the Song art of making tea.

(1012–1067) author of the *Record of Tea*, works which may be termed both detailed and exhaustive. In those times, methods of tea manufacture included pounding in bags and then rolling the tea into "pellets" or "sticks," thus giving rise to names such as "dragon and phoenix balls," "little dragon balls," "dense cloud dragon" and "dragon gliding in an auspicious cloud." By the time of the Xuanhe period, white colored tea was beginning to be valued. In the Song dynasty, Zheng Kejian, an official in charge of water transport, began to produce tea called "silver thread and ice bud" by pricking out the heart of the leaf, soaking it in clear spring water to eradicate "dragon's head" and other flavors (during the Song dynasty perfume was often added during the process of manufacturing tea) and pressing it into molds marked with a wriggling snake. At the time, the method known as "dragon ball defeating the snow" was regarded as immutable but what is esteemed in the present dynasty is not the same. The method of boiling is different and is simpler and more widely employed, and the natural charm is completely retained to the extent that it may be called the ultimate flavor of tea. As to the rinsing of dirt from tea leaves, the observation of the stages of boiling, the choice of tea utensils: these are many individual skills rather than the mere act of boasting about baskets for ash, vessels for containing water, bamboo wind stoves, or tubes of bamboo for containing tea(fig. 161).

Tiger Hill Tea and Heaven's Pond Tea

Tiger Hill tea from Suzhou is renowned for its quality and is the best there is. Unfortunately, the very little that is produced is acquired for official use. The hill folk of remote places may gather a jarful or two and regard it as a great rarity but in truth its flavor is not as good as *jie* tea. Heaven's Pond tea from the Longchi area of Suzhou is the best and the earliest is from the Southern Hills. It has a slight flavor of fresh grass.

Jie Tea

The *Jie* tea from Changxing in Zhejiang is the best. It is also very expensive and much valued by people today. *Jie* tea from Jingxi near Yixing in Zhejiang is slightly less good. Tea should not be picked when the buds are too slender as they will only just have sprouted and the flavor will lack body; nor should it be picked when it is too dark as by then it will be too old and the flavor will lack delicacy. It is best when stems have just appeared and the leaves are green and thickly curled. They should not be dried in the sun but cured over a charcoal fire and then cooled with a fan, wrapped in indicalamus leaf and stored high, away from the ground in an earthen jar, since tea prefers to be warm and dry and abhors cold and damp.

Liu'an Tea

This tea from Liuan in Anhui Province is suitable as a medicine but should not be heated as if frying since there will be no fragrance and the flavor will be bitter, though the quality of the tea itself is good.

Songluo Tea

Apart from several tens of *mu* of cultivation at Songluo Hill in Anhui Province, there is no true Songluo tea and there are only one or two families with the real skill in its preparation by heating. Today there are some Buddhist monks in the hills with great skill in heating it by hand. Genuine Songluo tea is not as good as Dongshan tea but better than Heaven's Pond tea. It is much appreciated by the people of Xin'an (present-day Chun'an County in Hangzhou of Zhejiang Province). It is very fashionable in the courtesan quarter of Nanjing since it is easy to brew and has a heavy fragrance.

---

1 Chen Zhi points out that *anxi* (安息) is the Chinese name for Parthia.

Fig. 162   Dragon Well Tea

The leaves of Dragon Well Tea are straight and smooth and a glossy green in color, with a sweet fragrance. The tea soup itself has a sweet crispness of taste. It has always been a speciality of Zhejiang Province.

Longjing Tea and Tianmu Tea

Longjing (Dragon Well) tea (fig. 162) from the Hangzhou West Lake and Tianmu (Eye of Heaven) tea from Mount Tianmu near Lin'an in Zhejiang Province both grow on hills where the cold comes early and there is much snow in winter, thus the tea sprouts rather late but if the picking and heating is done skillfully it is on a par with Heaven's Pond tea.

Rinsing Tea

To rid tea leaves of dirt, first rinse them in water that has boiled and then cooled slightly, then put them in a vessel from the Ding Kiln, wait until cool and then make tea, whereupon the fragrance will rise of itself.

Boiling Water

With water, a gentle fire heats and a living fire boils. A living fire is one where there is a flame from the burning wood. When the water begins to look like fishes eyes, this is the "first boil," when the edges bubble, it is the "second boil," and when the whole is a raging foam, it is the "third boil." Pouring the water when the wood has only just caught alight and the flames have just started and the water vapor has not yet evaporated is known as "tender." When the water has boiled overlong and the liquid has lost its character it is known as "old." In neither case is the fragrance of the tea released.

Rinsing Utensils

If the teapot and the tea bowls (fig. 163) are not clean, the flavor of the tea will be damaged. Tea utensils are ready for use after they have been washed and wiped with a clean cloth.

Tea Washers

Tea washers are made of clay. Shaped liked a large bowl they have an upper and lower compartment. The bottom of the upper compartment is perforated with a number of holes through which sand and dirt are carried away when the tea is strained. It is extremely convenient.

Tea Stoves and Hot Water Pots

There are tea stoves cast in bronze by Jiang bearing the face of a *taotie* and others that are completely plain, as well as some that

Fig. 163   Rabbit's Hair Tea Bowl from the Jian Kiln
Song dynasty
Height overall 6.5 cm, diameter at mouth 11.5 cm, diameter at foot 4.2 cm
Palace Museum, Taibei

Tea bowls are vessels from which to drink tea. They are generally smaller than rice bowls but bigger than wine cups and have a wide mouth and sloping sides. Tea bowls from the Jian Kiln at Jianyang in present-day Fujian Province have been famous for centuries and the rabbit's hair tea bowl is the kiln's archetypal product. The transparency of the black glaze reveals evenly distributed greenish-yellow striations, rather like the fine hair of a rabbit. When tea is made in one of these bowls there is an attractive mutuality of reflection between the tea and the hair pattern.

are cast in the form of tripod cauldrons or sacrificial wine vessels (*yi*). They can all be used. The best hot water pots are of lead with tin next, though those of bronze may also be used. Those in the shape of a bamboo pipe do not catch fire and are easy to pour. Porcelain pots have no effect on the flavor of the tea but should not be used, nor are they elegant in appearance.

Teapots and Tea Bowls

The best teapots are made of clay since clay does not affect the flavor even if tea is steeped in it for a long time. Pots made by Gong Chun are the most valuable but they are inelegant in form and lack small examples. Those made by Shi Dabin of this (Ming) dynasty are too small. The most useful are those that can hold half a *sheng* (about 500 ml) of water and are of simple, clean, ancient appearance and pour well (fig. 164). The common types known as "handled," "reclining melon," "double peach," "fan shaped," "eight-edged slender blossom," "tin handled," and "blue decoration on white ground" should not be used. The best teapots of tin, particularly for use during the winter, are made by Zhao Liangbi of Jiajing period. More recently, the teapots made by Gui Maode of Suzhou and Huang Yuanji of Jiahe (present-day Jiaxing in Zhejiang Province) are highly priced but both small and vulgar. Teapots of gold and silver are of no account.

The tea bowls with pointed feet made during the Xuanzong reign are of superior material quality and elegant appearance, they are thickly textured and do not lose heat and the jade-like pure white of their color assists in judging the color of the tea; they are the

Fig. 164 Purple Clay Teapot from Yixing

Qing dynasty
Height overall 8.5 cm,
diameter at mouth 5.4 cm,
diameter at foot 6.2 cm
Palace Museum, Beijing

This teapot has a round mouth, drum-like belly, circular foot and a short spout. The pale purple clay from which it is made contains granules of yellow. The body of the pot is smooth and plain and there is nothing out of place about the detailing. The artistry is consummate and although the piece bears a Qing reign-mark it still fully accords with Wen Zhenheng's ideal of "ancient design and construction."

very best. The mound-shaped tea bowls of the Jiajing period are used for both tea and wine and were inscribed "for use at the sacrificial altar of Daoist ceremony;" these are also excellent. Others such as "Ding Kiln white" may be collected but are not for daily use. It is as well to remember that in making tea, a cold bowl is made hot before the tea will froth and that vessels from old kilns are easily damaged thereby. There is also a kind of bowl from the "Cuigong" Kiln that is a little larger and in which fruit may be placed without affecting the fragrance of the tea, but only hazelnuts, pine nuts, fresh bamboo shoots, foxnuts and lotus seeds. Other kinds of fruit, such as tangerines, oranges, jasmine and osmanthus, should on no account be used.

The Choice of Wood

Tea abhors smoke. Thus charcoal must be used. Though fallen leaves, slivers of bamboo, tree twigs and pine cones make for topics of elegant conversation, they should really not be used. Moreover, wood that spits and oily or greasy wood will fill a chamber with smoke, the greatest enemy of tea. Charcoal from Tea Hill at Changxin called "golden charcoal," small or large and with wheat husks used as kindling, may be termed the friend of tea.

Fig. 165 *The Garden of the Humble Administrator*, Album Leaf
Wen Zhengming
Ink on paper
Height 26.4 × Width 27.3 cm
Metropolitan Museum of Art New York

Two scholars sit opposite each other surrounded by a number of tall trees, while on one side a boy attendant awaits orders.

TRANSLATOR'S NOTE

A translator frequently rides on the back of the work and wisdom of others. This is particularly so when the subject matter is specialized or exotic as it is in this case. The framework of essential knowledge necessary to support even an adequate translation of *Treatise on Superfluous Things*, Wen Zhenheng's late Ming guide to good taste, is beyond the immediate grasp of a non-specialist translator such as this one.

Fortunately help has been at hand, firstly in the basis of this translation, the scholarly Chinese edition of *Treatise* edited by Chen Zhi (1899–1989), a noted expert on garden design and Professor of Forestry at Nanjing Forestry University. This meticulously corrected and edited work was completed in 1965 but only published in 1984 just five years before his death in 1989. His footnotes have illuminated the obscurities of the text and all the botanical identifications in the translation are his. Where necessary, his footnotes are reproduced in the text. Because of the highly allusive nature of parts of the text, some editorial expansion has also been necessary. Instead of relegating these explanatory expansions to footnotes, they have been incorporated in the text. Dates have also been added.

Craig Clunas, Professor Emeritus of the History of Art, University of Oxford, has published extensively in this area over the years and anyone who ventures into this territory is immediately in his debt, a debt that in my case is impossible to repay. I have shamelessly plundered his scholarship for intellectual, political and technical background without, I hope, committing the sin of plagiarism, in China a lesser offence than failing to take account of the teachings of the past.

I have also relied upon other works to guide me through the maze of late Ming taste and fashion; *The Craft of Gardens*, Alison Hardie's impeccable translation of Ji Cheng's *Yuan Ye* and a shining model of illustration and presentation; Peter Valder's *The Garden Plants of China*, at the same time both comprehensive and precise; the monumental *Chinese Architecture* from the Yale University Press; and Endymion Wilkinson's *Chinese History: A New Manual*, a very backbone to any deep enquiry into the structures of the past in China.

The translator's engagement does not stop at the text, he spends time with the author and must read his mind and try to see and hear as he does, even at a distance of several hundred years. Wen Zhenheng emerges as an extremely fastidious man of wide knowledge and strong opinions and certainly, in his own view, of impeccable taste, but with an underlying yearning for simplicity and an instinctive feeling for the natural world, all combined with a deep distaste for ostentatious vulgarity. He does not represent a commonality of attitude but, rather, the views of the class of well-off gentlemen scholars and like them he clings to the sources of the past.

As ever, Wu Yuezhou in Shanghai has nurtured this book with indefatigable editorial guidance and support and saved me from egregious error. Diane Davies has edited the copy with skill and common sense. My debt of gratitude to them all has grown over the years. Without them this translation and a number of others would never have seen the light of day.

Tony Blishen
Lostwithiel—London—Kingussie

APPENDICES

Fig. 166 *Eighteen Scholars Screen* (detail, see page 12)

DATES OF THE CHINESE DYNASTIES

Xia Dynasty（夏）...2070–1600 BC
Shang Dynasty（商）...1600–1046 BC
Zhou Dynasty（周）...1046–256 BC
    Western Zhou Dynasty（西周）...1046–771 BC
    Eastern Zhou Dynasty（东周）...770–256 BC
        Spring and Autumn Period（春秋）...........................770–476 BC
        Warring States Period（战国）..................................475–221 BC
Qin Dynasty（秦）...221–206 BC
Han Dynasty（汉）..206 BC–AD 220
    Western Han Dynasty（西汉）..206 BC–AD 25
    Eastern Han Dynasty（东汉）...25–220
Three Kingdoms（三国）...220–280
    Wei（魏）..220–265
    Shu Han（蜀）...221–263
    Wu（吴）...222–280
Jin Dynasty（晋）...265–420
    Western Jin Dynasty（西晋）..265–316
    Eastern Jin Dynasty（东晋）..317–420
Northern and Southern Dynasties（南北朝）................................420–589
    Southern Dynasties（南朝）...420–589
    Liang Dynasty（梁）...502–557
    Northern Dynasties（北朝）..439–581
Sui Dynasty（隋）..581–618
Tang Dynasty（唐）...618–907
Five Dynasties and Ten Kingdoms（五代十国）............................907–960
    Five Dynasties（五代）..907–960
    Ten Kingdoms（十国）..902–979
Song Dynasty（宋）...960–1279
    Northern Song Dynasty（北宋）.......................................960–1127
    Southern Song Dynasty（南宋）.......................................1127–1279
Liao Dynasty（辽）..916–1125
Jin Dynasty（金）..1115–1234
Xixia Dynasty (or Tangut)（西夏）...1038–1227
Yuan Dynasty（元）...1279–1368
Ming Dynasty（明）...1368–1644
Qing Dynasty（清）...1644–1911

INDEX